FIFTY YEARS A FIGHTER

BARE-KNUCKLE CHAMPION OF THE WORLD

JEM MACE
CHAMPION OF THE WORLD

FIFTY YEARS A FIGHTER

BARE-KNUCKLE CHAMPION OF THE WORLD

JEM MACE

Peerless Press

First published 2014 by Peerless Press

Cover design by A. Schupmann

Internal illustrations by L.J. Karnes

Fifty Years A Fighter

Bare-Knuckle Champion of the World

Copyright this edition © Peerless Press

ISBN : 978-095703-422-8

All rights reserved

Published in Great Britain by Peerless Press

This edition Copyright © Peerless Press

Printed & bound in England

All rights reserved. No part of this book may be reproduced in any form by photocopying or any electronic or mechanical means, including information storage or retrieval systems, without permission in writing from both the copyright owner and the publisher of the book.

The right of Jem Mace to be identified as the author of this work has been asserted by him in accordance with the Copyright, Designs and Patents Act 1988 and any subsequent amendments thereto.

A catalogue record for this book is available from the British Library

An environmentally friendly book printed and bound in England by www.printondemand-worldwide.com

This book is made entirely of chain-of-custody materials

Contents

Introduction	11
Chapter 1: My Early Days	23
Chapter 2: I Leave Home	29
Chapter 3: Fiddle And I	35
Chapter 4: I Lose My Violin & Become a Professional Pugilist	43
Chapter 5: I Fight 'Farden' Smith & Join Nat Langham	51
Chapter 6: I Come to London	61
Chapter 7: I Go 'On the Spree'	67
Chapter 8: Matched to Fight Bill Thorpe	71
Chapter 9: I Am Disgraced	79
Chapter 10: A Friend In Need	87
Chapter 11: I Fight Sam Hurst	93
Chapter 12: Tom King's Challenge and some Reminiscences	105
Chapter 13: I Fight Tom King	119
Chapter 14: My Second Fight with Tom King	129

Chapter 15: Tom King Retires   139

Chapter 16: Prize-Fighters and the Law   151

Chapter 17: The Fight With Goss Comes Off   163

Chapter 18: A Fight Prevented in Ireland   173

Chapter 19: My Third and Last Fight with Joe
    Goss   183

Chapter 20: Tom Sayers and other Memories   195

Chapter 21: I Go to America   209

Chapter 22: I Fight Davis Twice and leave America
    for Australia   223

Afterword   233

Introduction

James or 'Jem' Mace must stand as one of the most fascinating characters in the history of the sport of boxing. Not only was Mace the last of the great British bare-knuckle masters and the very first champion of the world, he might also be considered to be the man chiefly responsible in having popularized modern boxing as a global sport from the ashes of the old English bare knuckle prize ring. Truthfully, there can be no man to whom the term the 'Father of Modern Boxing' could more honestly be applied than Jem Mace.

When Mike Tyson travelled to the United Kingdom to fight Julius Francis in the latter part of his career, the former two-time Heavyweight champion of the world was asked if he had the opportunity to meet one British person either living or dead, who would he choose. Tyson, an avid and lifelong student of boxing history, did not have to consider his answer for long, and replied Jem Mace, a blacksmith's son from Beeston, Norfolk, who had passed away the best part of a century previously. The name brought little recognition amongst the majority of those present, with the name of Jem Mace and his remarkable life story having largely been forgotten over the course of time.

No doubt, Mace for his part would have been equally intrigued to meet Tyson, the youngest man to have ever held the undisputed world heavyweight title with gloves, over a century after Jem himself won it - with bare knuckles, near a plantation in Louisiana.

Yet, for all the hard battles that Mace fought, he was much more than just a fighter. From his earliest days as a youth he had scratched his way as a musician, busking around the market towns and fairs of England, working as a performance artist, ceaselessly wandering in the company of other entertainers, travellers and Romany gypsies. His life was largely spent 'on the road', and Mace's charismatic bearing was such that he was equally at home whether rubbing shoulders with fellow pugilists, publicans, entertainers, circus performers, gypsies and even, as his career progressed, with Lords, ladies and future Presidents.

Mace was for many a fistic hero, celebrated amongst his fellow pugilists and the toast of the devotees of the prize ring known as 'the Fancy'. Yet his scandalous life, including his many love affairs, his multiple marriages, and his cunningness in the ring also ensured that he received his fair share of detractors who viewed him as nothing more than a charlatan, a womanizer, a trickster, and even, at one particularly dark juncture in Jem's life which was splashed across the sporting papers, as nothing more than an 'arrant cur' and a coward.

His relentless travelling continued throughout his professional life, and, by the time Mace was done swapping fists for prize money, he had claimed both the Middleweight and Heavyweight Championships of England, and the World title while in America. Aside from his own ring career he also succeeded in popularizing the sport of boxing in Australia, and, by doing so, brought a new generation of world champion boxers to the attention of the masses. In a lifetime of almost perpetual motion, Jem's fighting ability took him round the world at a time when the movements of the vast majority of his countrymen were restricted to just a few square miles. Mace travelled throughout Britain, touring the provinces as a star attraction by showcasing his skills at the circus and on the boxing booths. While in America he met opponents from New York to New Orleans. Wherever Mace went, be it Canada, Australia, New Zealand or South Africa, the Englishman was heralded as the greatest living exponent of his art, and his influence continued to be felt long after his retirement from competitive combat.

The face of pugilism was changed forever directly as a result of Mace's endeavors. When he had first entered the competitive prize ring, fighting was outlawed throughout the land; contests were often both bloody and brutal, and a fight comprised no set number of rounds. The use of bare knuckles frequently resulted in severe injury, horrific gashes and bloody facial wounds from sharp edged knuckles were commonplace. Attacks were launched without a truly scientific understanding of what type of blow might bring about a genuine knockout, and so the punishment might go on for an extended amount of time.

A round only ended when a man went down, with the fallen combatant having to be brought 'up to scratch' – a line marked in the centre of the ring, within a thirty second duration. The fighters would begin anew, until either unconsciousness occurred or the strength of one of the fighter's gave out. With no 'final' round, a contest was open ended and might conceivably go on for hours. Combatants often suffered terrible injuries as a result. Many fatalities were recorded down the years, often as a direct result of a man's backers refusing to concede that their fighter had been beaten, continuing to push him out of his corner to do battle, until inevitably at some point his body could take no more.

Throws and holds were also allowed, with there being no rules or regulations against falling on top of a victim and further crushing or winding him with your own bodyweight to finish him off. This also ensured that, to compete in the prize ring, a fighter also needed to have a keen knowledge of wrestling. Such dreadful throws as the 'cross-buttocks' often left a man unconscious on the ground, or in a heap of fractured limbs, with the hoarse cries of the spectators shouting 'fair fall !, a fair fall !' ringing in his ears.

With matches frequently leaving both the victor as well as the vanquished either battered or broken, the sport was outlawed, with the police on the lookout for well known offenders. Contests afterwards took place in secret, with the fighters and their supporters being forced to travel to more remote rural destinations to pitch a portable ring. A secluded spot with good turf was chosen, where a contest might be able to continue unmolested by the police, although prosecution by the authorities was not the only risk facing the combatants.

The old time pugilist was almost entirely dependent on the assistance of his backers to progress in the London Prize Ring (L.P.R. or P.R.). Without the support and money of well-heeled and well financed members of 'the Fancy' as the followers of the ring were known, a fighter had little chance of succeeding in reaching the heights of his pugilistic career. Unfortunately, with gambling being such an integral part of the prize fighting world, it also meant that in the event that a man was being beaten, his followers might stoop to any means to make sure that they did not lose their stake money. Many fights were marred by spectators choosing to break into the ring, and attacking the fighters or the referee, in order to 'win' the decision on behalf of their man, or at least succeed in bringing an abrupt end to the contest in the event that his defeat proved imminent.

With such rich pickings to be found amongst some elements in the crowd, in later years the prize ring became besieged by a motley selection of thieves, pickpockets, blackguards, garrotters, 'bludgeon men' and other dangerous characters. Inevitably, with the passing of time, even the most enthusiastic of spectators came to realize that attempting to witness a prize fight would mean rubbing shoulder with dubious characters who might well rob them of their valuables under threat of a beating or worse, and many devotees of the ring stayed away from a fight – that is, in the event a match came off at all. In the dying days of the prize ring it was not uncommon for a fight promoter, usually a publican of a sporting 'house' to have tickets printed for a contest, only for the fight to be abandoned, or for the police to be anonymously tipped off about an impending battle. Inevitably, the promoter cleaned up while washing their hands of the affair, and the punters lost their money.

The pugilistic world in which Mace began his fighting career bears little comparison with the one that he left behind. In time, bare fists had been replaced by gloves; a new system of rules had been introduced, which would become popularly known as the 'Marquis of Queensberry Rules', with these innovations having been promoted by Mace throughout his journeying around the globe. Mace would be amongst the first of those to congratulate 'Gentleman' Jim Corbett on becoming the first World Champion under Queensberry rules, which ushered in the new age of gloved combat, consigning the days of the organized bare knuckle prize ring to the history books once and for all. For Mace, Corbett's defeat of John L. Sullivan, the previous champion of America, was vindication of the principles of scientific boxing that he had helped introduce, and which ultimately triumphed over the rule of brawn, which had become so prevalent in the old prize ring.

In the modern age, contests would now take place in comfortable surroundings, indoors, and inside a permanent ring of set dimensions, unhampered by bad weather and changeable conditions underfoot. A canvas covered ring meant that the combatants no longer had to wear spiked shoes to assist them in holding their footing on wet, muddy, or slippery turf. Illumination by electric lighting also meant that a fighter no longer had to fear losing the coin toss for corners and end up further handicapped by the sun shining into their eyes while trying to engage an opponent in battle.

The fight itself was now strictly regulated and controlled by a referee, separated from, and unmolested by the spectators. Crucially, rounds were now three minutes in length, with a set interval of a minute between rounds. There were no more prolonged brawls, decreasing in ferocity over time as weariness and exhaustion set in. Wrestling or throwing was also no longer allowed, meaning that wrestlers with limited boxing ability were unable to gain advantage through cornering a superior opponent and crushing, flipping or falling on him until victory was secured.

In this way, boxing had ceased to be a sport where brute strength and physical endurance had become the overriding deciding factor in who might emerge victorious from a contest. This was in no small part due to the superior ring strategies and skills that Mace had himself showcased from his earliest years fighting in the P.R.

Adapting his methods to his adversaries, Mace perfected a style of boxing that initially appeared so unorthodox to spectators that he was accused of cowardice, such was the contrast between his methods and the more rough and ready tactics of his peers. Mace used strategy to outwit the clumsy movements and blows of his opponent in a manner that had not been seen in the prize ring prior to his time. By mastering the art of feinting, and combining this with side stepping, parrying and ducking,

Mace proved to be an elusive and difficult target, and about as well rounded a fighter that had ever graced the ring. Additionally, while Mace weighed in at just around eleven stone, he had a tremendously hard punch, and utilized a solid left jab, which he used to good effect in dismantling his opponent's defense, before unleashing the full and terrible power of his right hand to finish them off.

It was these skills that enabled Jem to remain more or less unmarked at the end of his long career in the ring, without the disfiguration to his facial features that had charted the ups and downs of so many others. The only indication that Mace had spent his days as one of the foremost ring men of his day was his knuckles, which naturally were smashed and broken from his many years fighting as a bare knuckle gladiator, with a great hump on the back of his hands testifying to the wear and tear that he had subjected them to over the course of many years.

The early life of Jem Mace provides a fascinating glimpse into life 'as it was' in rural England in the 1840's, in the days before organized sports, before football, and even before cricket, when the sporting life of the common man comprised little more than such homespun activities as cock-fighting, running, wrestling and bare knuckle fighting. The picture that Mace also paints of the final days of knuckle fighting bears no comparison with any other testament of his time. His memories from the darkest days of the prize ring are those of one who was there, and in the thick of it. It was Mace that would take with him his unsurpassed knowledge of ring craft to the distant corners of the globe, laying the foundation stones of organized glove boxing in the 'new' world, just as England was turning its back on bare knuckle pugilism forever.

Beyond its significance as a historical record charting the final days of prize-fighting and the development of boxing, Jem Mace's *'Fifty Years A Fighter'* is a fantastic tale told by one of the most colourful characters to have ever graced the ring, whose skill, natural charisma and showmanship took him from the backwaters of rural England to the heights of international fame. Jem Mace was one of the greatest British fighters, not only one of the most influential figures to have 'toed the scratch' in the dying days of the old London Prize Ring, but also the man to whom most is owed in the creation of the modern sport enjoyed today by fans around the world. Undeniably, Jem Mace was the 'Father of Boxing'.

Prepare to be thrilled....

Lawrence Davies

Fifty Years A Fighter
The Life Story of Jem Mace

Chapter 1
My Early Days

I was born at the little village of Beeston, Norfolk, on April 8th, 1831, and was the son of one of four brothers, all blacksmiths.

Their names were Tom Mace, James Mace, William Mace and Barney Mace. William Mace was my father, and Barney Mace, my uncle, was the father of my cousin and great chum, Pooley Mace.

Pooley, I should like to explain here, was half a Romany, his father having fallen in love with and married a gipsy girl at Norwich Fair. Possibly this circumstance, coupled with the fact that Pooley was constantly with me for many years in circuses and boxing-booths, may have given rise to the assertion, oft-times repeated, that I have gipsy blood in my veins.

This statement is quite untrue. My ancestors, so far as I have been able to trace them, and that is for more than three hundred years back, have been British born, and were all, or nearly all, what country folk call 'tradesmen'; that is to say, they followed trades, being mostly wheelwrights, carpenters, or blacksmiths.

I myself was brought up to the anvil, or, rather, my father attempted so to bring me up. But one day, when I was about ten years old, I hit my thumb a whopping whack with the hammer, which I then threw down in disgust, declaring that I would have no more of it.

My father cuffed me soundly, and that not once nor twice only, but again and again. However, he found that I was as obstinate as he was. He couldn't cuff out of me the determination to do no more blacksmithing. So after a while he decided to let me alone.

Followed, a time of riotous freedom. I had never had any book-learning to speak of, for, of course, there were no board-schools in those days. Neither had I had, at that time, any religious instruction whatever, although our cottage adjoined a little chapel so closely that I could hear the minister preaching as I lay in bed on a Sunday morning.

I am afraid, however, that the words of the good man made but little impression on me. Not that I was viciously inclined. On the contrary, I had a reputation of being a rather well-disposed lad. But I was full of animal life and high spirits. These had to have an outlet. And, as a matter of course, the outlet was in fighting, my opponents being the other village lads of about my own age and weight.

I say 'as a matter of course', because at that time fighting was the one recreation of all classes. Neither cricket nor football existed then, in the sense that they do now, nor had the gentlefolks taken up with polo or golf. Consequently, all the interest that is now spread over these, and other sports, was concentrated on boxing.

Everybody learned to use his fists in those days; rich and poor, gentle and simple. Fighting was the one thing talked about. Every little village possessed its 'champion', and these used to meet one another, usually on Sunday, and fight to the finish with naked fists.

I remember there was an old barn about a mile out from Beeston, to which the 'fancy men' of the surrounding villages used to come to settle who was best. The battles I have seen in that barn! Why, some of them would not have discredited the regular ring.

Another favourite place for fighting was the 'Ploughshare Inn', Beeston. One could always be sure of seeing a fight there on a Saturday night. Not a quarrelsome fight, you understand. But just a ding-dong battle to decide which was the better man.

And they were battles, too, in those days. The 'knock out' blow had, of course, not been invented. So the two combatants simply hammered each other till one cried 'enough', or fell insensible by reason of the succession of blows rained on him by his opponent.

Some of the fiercest fights I have ever seen, outside the Prize Ring, were fought by young fellows of seventeen, or thereabouts, for the possession of the lasses. A village lad, in those days, stood little chance of getting a sweetheart that was worth having unless he was able to use his fists. The prettiest girls went to the hardest hitters. This was regarded so much as a matter of course, by both the girls and the boys, that I have repeatedly seen one of the former stand patiently by while two of the latter fought for her, and then, when the contest was finished, walk off quietly with the victor.

These 'love' fights, as we called them, used almost invariably to take place outside the 'Ploughshare', and this stood right opposite our cottage, so that I was able to get a good view of them from my bedroom window. The stocks, too, I remember, were close handy, and there was generally somebody in them on Saturday night. The prisoner also got a good view, for the crowd, always sympathetic and good-natured, used to keep a clear space for him to see the 'fun', besides supplying him with beer and 'bacca.

All this, no doubt, sounds very shocking to modem ears. And so, in a sense, possibly it was. But we saw nothing wrong in it. On the contrary, we revelled in it, and when we found a 'good lad', by which was meant a clever fighter, we all aimed to do likewise.

As for myself, I think the fighting instinct must have been extra strong in me, for before I was turned fourteen I had fought at least a score of battles. One, I recall, was with a big lad of nearly sixteen. We fought twenty rounds, and I got beat. He was the youngest of seven brothers, all of whom were chimneysweeps, and all noted bruisers. Well, I was wild and ashamed at having been licked, although I need not have been, for the other lad was older and bigger and stronger then I. But as I say, I *was* wild, and I *was* ashamed.

So what did I do but strut up one Sunday morning to where he and his six elder brothers were standing, and tell him in so many words that I intended, as soon as I grew big enough, to fight the lot of them, and beat them. Of course, they roared with laughter. But I meant what I said. And in after years I showed them that I meant it. For I challenged them one after the other, and beat them, too, soundly.

But I am running ahead, I find, too fast. I was eighteen or nineteen when I fought and thrashed the seven sweeps. And my first fight with the youngest of them in which I was defeated, took place when I was not yet fourteen.

A day or two afterwards, when I was still raw and sore from the battle, my father packed me off to Wells, in Norfolk, to a man named Fox, who had promised to teach me the cabinet-making trade.

Chapter 2
I Leave Home

It was the first time I had ever left home for any length of time, and I cried bitterly. My mother cried, too, I remember, and got up early in the morning to boil me some bacon and dumplings for my dinner on the road, for I was to perform the journey on foot.

All the village lads turned out to see me start, and to wish me good luck, and amongst them were many I had fought with. But we bore no enmity to one another, nor thought of doing so. No more than nowadays a man would think of bearing enmity to a friend that happened to beat him at golf.

I took with me a little bundle of clean clothes tied in a red cotton handkerchief, and carried at the end of a stick. Another handkerchief, of blue cotton, contained my bacon and dumplings. And under my arm, in a green baize bag, I carried my violin.

This latter had been given to me on my tenth birthday by an old sailor who lodged with us for a time. He told us he got it from Cremona, and that it was valuable. Very likely he spoke the truth. Anyway, it lives in my memory to this day as being the sweetest-toned instrument I ever played on, and I have handled some scores.

I suppose I had a natural gift for music. Indeed, I know I had. For before I was twelve I had learned to perform upon it very creditably, and that without ever having been taught, for the old sailor who gave it to me died shortly afterwards.

The possession of that old fiddle opened up a new life to me. It showed me that there was something to live for in the world other than fighting. I could not read. I could not write. I was ignorant with an ignorance of which the modern board-school boy can have no conception. But I found that I could draw from it sweet sounds that thrilled my whole being, and I was the better for it.

Just now I wrote that I was never taught to play it. But, on reflection, I think this is wrong. I *was* taught, and the wild things of the air and the woodlands were my teachers. I would get up at dawn, go out into the fields, and tune my violin to the song of the lark, the call of the cuckoo, the love cries of the moor fowl, the boom of the bittern. So, perhaps, I have thought since, was music first born.

But to return to my story. Behold me on this sunny summer morning, trudging merrily along the dusty road. Yes, merrily. For the pang of the parting was over. And, boylike, I longed to see fresh scenes. But the way was long, and towards the afternoon I grew a little weary. So, to cheer myself up a bit, I drew forth my violin and commenced to play.

I was still playing when I reached my destination, and presented myself before my new employer, Mr. Fox, who, I should explain, besides being a cabinet-maker was also a publican. At his request, I went through my entire repertoire, winding up with an improvised piece I used to call my 'cuckoo solo', in which I mimicked all the birds of the air, the cuckoo's note being made to sound in over and over at intervals.

When I had finished, Mr. Fox gave me so hearty a slap on the back that nearly all the breath was driven out of my body.

'What!' he shouted delightedly, 'you come here to learn to be a cabinet-maker when you can play the violin like that. Not if I know it. Here, you go up to the club-room'.

This club-room, I soon discovered, was the nightly resort of half the sailors and smugglers along the Norfolk coast, and it became my duty to play for them, they rewarding me with coppers or silver, as they felt inclined, with an occasional gold piece thrown in. The name of Mr. Fox's house was the 'Green Dragon', and I got nicknamed the 'Red Dragon' because of a flaming red guernsey I wore at the time.

This name annoyed me, for I considered it ridiculous, and I was very sensitive to ridicule, as indeed I think are most boys. The result was, of course, more fights, in which I was sometimes beaten, sometimes the victor, but in all of which I gained something of skill and adroitness in the use of my fists - skill and adroitness which were to stand me in good stead in after life, when I was to be called upon to wrest the world's championship from its then holder, and to maintain my right to it against some of the cleverest and gamest fighters on earth.

So the days and nights passed by. Days and nights of revelry and riot, interspersed with periods of perfect quietude, when the patrons of the 'Green Dragon' were away pursuing their respective callings. It was during one of these lulls in the usual routine that my master, seeing I had nothing to do just then in the way of either fiddling or fighting, set me to saw a number of great tree trunks that had just come down from Holcombe Hall.

The day was broiling hot. The job none to my liking. I made up my mind to run away.

Watching my opportunity I slipped upstairs to the garret where I slept, hastily gathered together my few belongings, including, of course, my beloved violin, and hied me off to the sea-shore. I lay there hidden amongst the sand-dunes for the rest of the day, and for the greater part of the short summer night, and just before dawn set out to walk the twenty odd miles that separated me from my father's house.

I arrived there, after an absence of fifteen months, just as the family were sitting down to breakfast. They looked surprised and father grumbled a bit, but on the whole I think they were glad to see me.

As for me, I tried to settle down to regular work, helping about the smithy, and so on. But I soon found it was impossible. So one day, before the others were astir, I took my fiddle under my arm, and set out into the world to seek my fortune.

Chapter 3
Fiddle And I

I was now between fifteen and sixteen years old, a fine, sturdy lad, well set up, clean of limb and sound of wind. I looked to my violin for a living, and it did not fail me. I wandered with it for company pretty well all over East Anglia, playing for coppers outside public-house doors, at gentlefolks' houses, at fairs and circuses; anywhere, in fact, where I thought there was a chance of my being suitably rewarded.

My best harvests, however, were, I soon discovered, reaped at the fairs, of which there were, in those days, a great number. These were frequented by large numbers of gipsy showmen, as well as horse-dealers; pig-jobbers, and so on. To all of these I soon became well-known, and many is the Romany merrymaking I have been asked to, my musical efforts always well rewarded. At gipsy weddings I was in great request, and I seldom netted less than a sovereign on such an occasion, all the guests contributing something.

Frequently, too, I would attach myself, for a week or a fortnight at a time, to someone amongst the many boxing booths that then were to be found at all fairs, and between the intervals of fiddling I would spar exhibition bouts with the gloves. These kept me fit, and gave me practice.

I needed both, for fights in real earnest were a regular part and parcel of my daily life. Many of these battles had their origin in jealousy. The horse-dealers at the fairs, finding I could ride, used to entrust me with colts to break in, and also employed me to ride their horses before possible purchasers, in order to show off their points. For this they would pay me from half-a-crown to five shillings a time.

This money, before I appeared on the scene, used to go to the gipsy boys themselves, and naturally they did not like it. I should think I fought between twenty and thirty battles from this one cause alone within the space of six or eight months. At the end of that time, however, my reputation was established, and none dared, or at all events, none cared, to challenge my right to earn as much money as I could, how and when I pleased.

I was up to all sorts of dodges for doing this. One was to volunteer to act as 'snuffer boy' at any circus that came along. A snuffer boy, I should explain, was a lad whose sole duty it was to go round the show during the evening performance and snuff the hundreds of tallow dips that in those days formed the only illuminant.

Then, of course, I was always ready to box for a purse with any lad of my own size and weight, or even a little bigger and heavier; I was not too particular. The 'purse', I may say, was usually a copper one if the bout was with gloves, silver if the bare fists were used. But even in the latter case it seldom exceeded eight or ten shillings in value.

And for this small sum two powerful, strapping lads, skilled boxers both, were expected to hammer one another until one or the other gave in or was knocked senseless. Nor did it do for the beaten one to give in too easily. If he did, the chances were that he would receive a sound basting from one or more of the aggrieved spectators, who considered that they had not received value for their money. On the other hand, if the contestants put up a game fight, the purse was often largely increased by contributions thrown into the ring, and not infrequently a separate purse would be subscribed for the loser.

These improvised prize-fights - for that is what they really were - used to take place in public-houses, usually in a club-room or skittle-alley. Sometimes the landlord would put up the entire purse, say half a sovereign, and charge threepence each for admission. In such cases we made a good thing out of it, for the

Jem on the road

spectators would almost always throw something into the ring in addition.

It will doubtless seem strange to this generation that goings on of this sort should have been allowed. Nowadays, of course, it would not be tolerated for an instant that licensed premises should be made the scene of a fight for money with the naked fists. But in the times I am writing of nobody seemed to see anything wrong in it.

Indeed, it was no uncommon thing for the squire himself, whose duty it was, if anybody's, to stop such exhibitions, to drop in at the village 'pub' when an unusually 'preety' fight was expected to come off. I have seen the parson, too, come in along with him, all fresh and ruddy from a long day's fox-hunting. They cheered and clapped with the best of the rustics, and we felt like cheering, too, for we knew that when the 'gentry' were present it meant an extra half-crown, or perhaps a crown if we put forth our best efforts. And this, I need hardly say, we never failed to do.

I am dwelling upon this portion of my life, partly because it is fresh in my memory, far fresher, in fact, than many later and more important events, but also because it will help the reader to understand much of what will come after. Indeed, I will go further than this. If the reader will take the trouble to throw himself properly into the spirit of the events, and the times I have tried to portray, he will grasp the whole meaning of the art and science of British boxing, as it was understood by his forefathers.

For in this same rough-and-tumble school that I was trained, were trained all the great exponents of the fistic art who preceded me and were my contemporaries - Jem Belcher, Bendigo, Gully, Tom Sayers, Tom Spring, Joe Goss, Mendoza, Tom King, Bob Brettle, and many others whose names I cannot now recall.

Fighters had to be fighters in those days. We fought for our lives, as it were. No drawing-room fighting. How can a man like Tommy Burns, for instance, who never fought a prize-fight in his life, and who would not be permitted by the authorities to fight one even if he wanted to ever so much, expect to vie with men of the old school, who were at it with the 'raw 'uns' as soon as they could walk almost?

Yet there were times, I must confess, when all this fighting palled upon me. I felt I had a stomach-full, and to spare. Perhaps I had been beaten two or three times running, a thing which did happen occasionally, for naturally I did not always come off the victor. Or it may have been that I simply felt the need for rest and change, a feeling that comes to all of us, even the youngest and lustiest, at times.

Anyway, these quiet fits did come over me occasionally, and it was then my custom to quit the fairs, and the towns and villages where I was known, and strike out into the remote country districts, playing my violin as I went, not refusing coppers if they were given me, but not going out of my way to seek them either. Indeed, I would often lie all day on my back in the woods, or far out on the open fen, remote from any habitation. Only when at the end of my resources, and threatened with the pangs of hunger, would I seek the towns again.

Chapter 4
I Lose My Violin & Become a Professional Pugilist

It was on one occasion such as this that an event occurred which, although I did not know it at the time, was destined to shape my whole after-career.

I had been tramping the country in the manner I have attempted to describe for two and a half years, and was consequently about eighteen years old. A fine, strapping lad I was, hard as iron, and as fit as my own fiddle.

I weighed between ten and eleven stone, and don't suppose there was an ounce of superflous flesh on me. I hardly knew my own strength, as the saying is. As an illustration of how tremendous were my hitting powers, even at this time, I may mention that I would frequently, for a small wager, drive my fist clean through the inch-thick wooden panel of a public-house door, after having first, of course, obtained the landlord's consent.

Well, as I was saying, it chanced that during one of these country rambles of mine, I found myself run out alike of money and food, and, in order to obtain some of both, I made my way to the nearest town, which chanced to be Yarmouth.

When I arrived there, following my usual custom, I stationed myself outside a public-house near the quay and tuned up my violin.

Hardly had I started playing, however, when out came three fishermen, and one of them, a big, hulking fellow, six feet tall, lifted a fist like a shoulder of mutton, and bringing it down on my poor little instrument, dashed it to the ground and smashed it all to pieces.

For the moment I was dumbfounded. Then the anger surged up in me. If he had broken my leg or arm I should not have minded so much. But my fiddle! Well, I know what I meant to do. Yes, if it cost me my life.

Yet outwardly I was quite calm.

I walked quietly up to the fellow, for he had jumped back the moment after he had broken my violin, and was out of arm's reach.

'Why did you do that?' I asked.

My answer was a volley of coarse jeers, punctuated with boisterous laughter, in which his two companions joined heartily.

'All right', I said, 'you've had your fun; now you're going to pay for it; look to yourself.'

The man stared, then laughed uneasily. A curious crowd gathered.

As for me, I gave one glance downwards to where, at my feet, lay my shattered violin, broken, I could see, beyond repair. Then I gritted my teeth, threw myself into fighting attitude, and cried to him once again to look to himself.

By this time he had realised I was in earnest. He put up his fists and at it we went.

Never in my life did I fight so gladly, or with feelings of more bitter animosity. He had smashed my fiddle, my one possession that I cared for more than aught else, and I meant smashing him.

I did, too, and it didn't take me long. In less than a quarter of an hour he was glad to cry 'enough', and slunk away, all bruised and bleeding, amidst the jeers of the bystanders.

Then I challenged the next biggest of his companions.

'All right', he replied, ' I'll fight thee, lad, but take a breathing spell first'.

'I want no breathing spell', I retorted, for I was mad with passion, you understand. 'Look to yourself'.

And with that we went at it. He proved a tougher nut to crack, though, than the other fellow had done, although he was a shorter man by a head and a good bit lighter. We went at it hammer and tongs for, I should think, a good half-hour, while the crowd cheered itself hoarse.

Nor would he give me best, as his mate had done, but kept on fighting, even after I had completely closed up one of his eyes, and very nearly served the other the same way. At last, however, I got in a knockdown blow straight from the shoulder, and he toppled over backwards, with his arms spread out like the sails of a windmill.

I heard his skull go 'crack' as it struck the cobblestones, and there he lay, stunned into insensibility.

Nevertheless, I felt no pity for him; only a great exultation. Neither was my anger sated. I turned to the last of the three.

'Look here', I said, 'I want a breathing spell now, for I am about winded. But in ten minutes by the clock look to yourself, for I'm going to have a go at you'.

The fellow, however, had no stomach for a fight, and commenced to whine excuses.

'I didn't break your fiddle', he said.

'I know you didn't', I replied. 'But you stood by and saw your mate break it, and you laughed at me and jeered at me after it was done, and now you've got to fight me'.

'All right', he said, sullenly, and walked to the outskirts of the crowd, at the same time making as if he was going to take his coat off and give it somebody to mind. Instead of doing so, however, he suddenly made a break, and before I knew where I was he was running like a deer down the quay side in the direction of Caister.

I took after him as soon as I had recovered from my surprise, and I doubt not I would have caught him despite the start he had - for I was a splendid sprinter in those days - but for my being winded with fighting.

As it was he got clean away, and I could have cried with vexation. I felt that I was being cheated out of one-third of my just revenge.

When I got back to the scene of my double encounter, I found that the man who I had knocked out was sitting up, and appeared to be recovering, for which I was not sorry, for I feared for his life. Not from any blow I had struck him, you will understand, but from the crack he got when he fell backwards on the stones.

Another thing that helped raise my spirits was the fact of the crowd having taken up a collection for me, to help me buy a new violin. This amounted altogether to something over two pounds. I was just moving off with this, after thanking them all for their kindness, when up came a gentleman, a real swell, and pressed a sovereign into my hand.

At the same time he looked me up and down steadily, as though running over my points.

'My', he exclaimed, after he had finished his inspection. 'My, but you're a well-plucked 'un, my lad. You ought to be a prize-fighter'.

Then he turned away and strode off. But he had said the words,

'You ought to be a prize-fighter!'

It was as though he had said to me you ought to be a king.

Indeed, to be a prize-fighter was in my estimation at that time a far more desirable thing than being a king. For I had never seen any kings, and knew nothing of them. Whereas I had seen plenty of prize-fighters, and knew that they were honoured above all other men, and flattered and petted, and made much of by the highest in the land.

Be a prize-fighter! Of course I would be a prize-fighter. Why not? How foolish of me not to have thought of it before!

That night I finally made up my mind. I would enter the ring, come what would.

So that is how I became a professional pugilist. Through a smashed violin.

But then came another question. How could I become a prize-fighter?

I knew nothing of London; I had never been there. And I was aware that it was in London, only in London, that backers were to be found.

I turned the matter over in my mind many times, and once I was nearly starting to tramp there, and chance my luck. Then I reflected that I knew not a soul in all that great city, and the prospect daunted me.

I was not frightened of the country and its loneliness. I had been accustomed to it from a child. And as for the towns and villages of East Anglia, I knew them by heart. But London! That was another matter.

So in the end I decided to go on pretty much as I had been going, only keeping always in view what I had made up my mind to do. I joined partnership with an old showman named 'Bunny' Blythe, and together we toured the Fen Country.

Chapter 5
I Fight 'Farden' Smith & Join Nat Langham

Meanwhile, fights continued as plentiful as they ever had been. Only I no longer fought in public-houses for a few shillings. I had grown to manhood now, or, at all events, I considered that I had, and I had, besides, achieved a local reputation of a sort, so deemed such boyish contests beneath me.

I fixed £5 as a minimum, below which I would not fight, and let it be known all through the fairs and markets of East Anglia that I was prepared to take on all comers at that price, or up to £10. I got some takers, but not a great many, for the stakes were considered 'big money' at that time, and in those parts.

Amongst others, I remember, was a man named Sydney Smith. He was a native of Wisbech, and a boxer of some reputation locally. The betting was in his favour. But I beat him, after a hard battle lasting nearly two hours.

Another local bruiser I met and defeated was Charlie Pinfold, of Norwich. We fought on Norwich Hill for a purse of £10. I should think that fully five hundred people assembled at this battle, expecting to see a big fight, for my previous encounter with Smith had made some stir. However, they were disappointed, for I knocked him out easily in the fourth round.

After that I received a challenge from a man called 'Farden' Smith. He was known as the King of the Gipsies, and was a regular giant, standing 6ft 2in in his stocking feet, and broad in proportion. Like my fight with Pinfold, this was brought off on Norwich Hill. Or rather, I should say, that it was attempted to be brought off, for we made the grand mistake of choosing market-day, and the crowds were so tremendous, and the obstruction they caused so great, that the police swooped down upon us after we had fought four or five rounds, and we had to take to our heels to escape being arrested.

He ran one way and I another, but we met later in the day and arranged to fight again at nine the next morning on Mousehill (pronounced 'Muzzle') Heath. This was where the gipsies' encampment was pitched, and I anticipated a rough time, so I took with me my old 'pal', Bob Bunn of Norwich, and a man nicknamed 'Friday', both good boxers and all-round athletes.

I need not have been alarmed, however, for when we got to the Heath, on the stroke of nine, as arranged, 'Farden' Smith absolutely declined to renew the contest. 'I give you best', Jem', he cried out, as he saw us approaching, 'but if either Friday or Bunn wants a fight, why, I'm their man!' As however, this was not what they had come out for, they declined; and the upshot of it was that we spent the rest of the day (it was Sunday) in dancing and merrymaking, I sending a gipsy wench back for my fiddle and providing the music.

My, what a day that was, to be sure! The gipsies were all in their best attire; the men in velveteen coats and knee-breeches, with white silk stockings, and shoes adorned with big paste buckles; the girls and young women in silks of all the colours of the rainbow, and wearing an abundance of jewellery that flashed and sparkled in the sunshine. All day long we danced and sang, and then sang and danced again, until the sun sank to rest, and the big round harvest moon came out above the scattered pine-trees, flooding all the purple heath with white radiance.

I fought several other fights for money besides these I have mentioned, perhaps ten or a dozen in two years. They were prize-fights in reality, although they did not count as such in the annals of the Ring, not being recorded in 'Fistiana', which is the prize-fighter's Almanach de Gotha.

For this reason I tried hard to get in touch with some of the London men, but for a long time in vain. Then, one day when I was giving an exhibition of sparring in a booth at Norwich Fair, in walked a fine, strapping fellow, elegantly dressed, with a big hard face, clean-shaven, and a look about him that told me in an instant he was one of the 'fancy'.

He stood and watched me critically for a while, then he came over and shook hands.

'You're Jem Mace', he said.

'Yes', I replied, wondering all the while who he could be and what he wanted with me.

'You don't know me?' was his next remark.

'No, I don't', I replied.

'Well', he said, 'I'm Nat Langham, and I've heard of you. Would you like to take a situation in my boxing booth?'

Now, I don't suppose the name of Nat Langham means much to the men of this generation. But in those days there was no more influential or famous man connected with the ring. His triumphs were many, and they had been blazoned all over England. For one thing, he was the only man who ever beat Tom Sayers. This he did on October 18th 1853 at Lakenham, after a terrific contest lasting sixty rounds. Sayers was stone blind at the finish, and Nat himself was so dreadfully punished about the body, it was thought for some time that his life was in danger.

He recovered, however, and, having retired from the ring, settled down as a sporting publican at a place called the Cambrian Stores, in St. Martin's Lane, London. Here he founded the Rum-pum-pas Club, an association of aristocratic patrons of the ring. This gave him immense influence; in fact, he had for a time the monopoly of the business side of pugilism, because a novice could hardly ever hope to get at the right men to back him except through Nat's recommendation.

Besides the Rum-pum-pas, he also ran a boxing booth which travelled the country, and was considered the best thing of its kind on the road. The ordinary booths charged threepence admission, and sixpence for the reserved seats. The prices at Nat's were half a crown and five shillings. But for this he put before his patrons the best talent in England, fighters who, it was clearly understood, were little if any beneath championship form.

Now you know about this, you will understand something of what Nat's invitation to join his company meant to me. Of course, I accepted gladly, not even enquiring as to terms, which I found afterwards were £2 a week and 'all found'.

For this I had to meet all comers with the gloves, and beat them, for Nat had no use for a boxer who allowed himself to be defeated. One

Mace joins Nat Langham's troupe

lost battle, or at most, two, meant instant dismissal. But on this point I had no misgivings.

Behold me then, on the morning following the eventful meeting, strutting about the fair as vain as any peacock, clad in a brand new guernsey of the regulation pattern, the mittens on my hands, all ready, nay eager, to do battle on behalf of my patron. It was, indeed, the proudest moment of my life. They could hardly persuade me to take off either gloves or guernsey, even when night fell. Already, I saw myself in imagination fighting for the championship before the London 'swells'. I simply longed to prove my mettle under the critical eyes of 'Ould Nat' himself.

Nor did I have long to wait. For during the very first week of my engagement, my employer took me with him to Horncastle Fair, where I was matched with the gloves against a local champion, whose name I forget. He was a celebrity, though, in his way, for I recollect that the booth was packed, although the wily Nat, who ever had his eye on the main chance, had put up the prices of admission by one-half.

When he entered the ring I saw at once that I was going to have a tough job, for he was a much bigger and heavier man than I, with a face as hard as a marble mantelpiece. Indeed, one of his mates told me afterwards that they could break a stick across his 'jib' without leaving a mark. However, I defeated him, after a tremendous struggle, the battle lasting nearly two hours, and ending in the other man being licked to a standstill.

Langham was so pleased at my success that he made a match for me to fight a man named Jack Pratt of Norwich for £10 with the naked fists. But this time luck was against me. My hands gave out; and at the end of fifty rounds, as I could not close them, and as the fight, so far as I was concerned, had resolved itself into a slapping match, my seconds threw up the sponge.

Nat was exceedingly angry at my failure, especially when he found that I had undergone no proper training, and had made no attempt to pickle my hands. 'Next time you are going in for a real fight with the raw 'uns, do both', he said curtly, and turned on his heel.

I remembered his advice, and acted on it, with the result that my next encounter ended in my favour. This was with a man named Slack, the stakes being £5 a side, and the date October 2nd, 1855. The battle took place at Mildenhall, near Newmarket, and was the last prize-fight ever held at this place, once the favourite resort, above all others in England, for these encounters.

The battle was a comparatively tame affair, I beating my man in nine rounds, lasting nineteen minutes only. But it was noteworthy in another way, for it was chronicled in 'Fistiana', so that with it begins my official connection with the ring.

John Slack, who Mace beat in nine rounds

Chapter 6
I Come to London

So elated was Nat with my success, that he insisted on my accompanying him to town, with a view to my giving exhibitions of my skill before his aristocratic patrons of the Rum-pum-pas.

I remember, as though it were yesterday, my first introduction to this famous club. It was on a Wednesday, the day when the reunions invariably took place. The members had just dined in a large upper room of Nat's commodious hostelry, the centre of which was roped off with stakes like a regular prize ring. Within this mock ring the table was set, the viands being then, as always, roast beef and plum pudding, with, of course, the proper 'garnishings', and any amount of 'lashings', in the shape of port wine, champagne, and brandy.

Nat, who acted as a sort of master of the ceremonies, introduced me as a 'novice from the country'. I was not invited to partake of the feast; indeed, the eating part of it was all over by the time I entered the room. But several of the members rose and shook hands with me, saying they had heard of me as a game fighter and a candidate for championship honours, and wishing me good luck.

At the time, of course, I did not know who any of these gentlemen were. But I got to know the majority pretty well in after years, and amongst those who were present, and who greeted me so kindly, were, I remember, Lord Drumlanrig, Lord Caledon (afterwards Lord Verulam), his brother, the Hon. 'Bob' Granston, Lord Edward Russell, Sir Edward Kent, the Hon. 'Billy' Duff, and Mr. Keen, of mustard fame.

I was offered champagne and brandy, but refused both, for I felt somehow that this was to be the turning point of my career, and, besides, I was never a lover of strong drink. And well was it for me, for my mettle was tried that day, if ever it was.

As soon as the table was cleared away, the 'fun' began. First, Lord Drumlanrig stepped into the ring from which all the diners had by this time withdrawn, and, bowing gracefully to me, asked if 'Mr. Mace would oblige him with a few rounds'.

Of course, I had no choice in the matter, and even if I had had I should have been only too delighted. So we donned the mittens, and at it we went. There was no sparring for points in those days. His lordship went for me with all he knew, and I did the same as regards him.

I was stripped to the buff, as was the custom with the 'pros' at these contests, but Lord Drumlanrig wore a fine ruffled shirt, and this was soon smothered in his blood and well-nigh torn to ribbons besides. Yet he fought determinedly on, trying to give me as good as I was giving him, but quite without success.

Nevertheless, he did not show the slightest trace of anger all through, but fought on and on, with a smile on his pale handsome face, like the game Briton he was. And when at last he had to give me best, he shook me by the hand, and, pulling out a couple of sovereigns, asked my acceptance of them, with many kind and flattering words.

Then he turned to Langham, and said, 'Nat, your "novice" is too good for me; better set one of your "pros" at him'. 'All right, your lordship', cried Nat, and in a trice I found myself confronting Johnny Walker, a famous old-time pugilist, whose victorious battles in the ring with Fred Mason, Sam Simmonds, Ned Adams, and others had made his name known all over England. He was twelve or thirteen years older than me, though, and I had it all my own way from the first, beating him in less than half an hour by the clock.

Then, after I had a wash and a dish of tea, they set a man named 'Mo' Betson on to me and, when I had beaten him, yet another, whose name I forget, but whom I served likewise. This made four men I had defeated in the one day, and the swells cheered me and prophesied all sorts of good of me, winding up by subscribing a purse which amounted altogether to some £5, not counting the two sovereigns I had from Lord Drumlanrig.

Mace beat four men one after another at the Rum-pum-pas Club

Chapter 7
I Go 'On the Spree'

That evening I felt as if I was walking on air. My future, I considered, was assured. And the cup of my happiness was filled to overflowing when, towards ten o'clock, 'Bob' Grunston, 'Billy' Duff, and two or three more of the swells, chose me as their 'bodyguard' for a 'night out' in the West End.

This needs some explanation, for young aristocrats of the present day do not dream of hiring professional pugilists to accompany them when sallying forth for a spree. But, then, the London of today is not as was the London of the middle fifties. Then there was some danger, if not to life, certainly to limb, where now is perfect safety.

So, in order to be on the safe side, whenever a party of Nat's 'young bloods' sallied forth to 'see life', after nightfall, the thoughtful Nat provided a 'pug' or two, whose faces were familiar to the 'boys', as a 'bodyguard'. The 'pug's' remuneration for this service, I may add, was a guinea, and this was duly paid me at starting. With me, as my colleague, was the 'Mo' Betson alluded to above, Nat rightly arguing that although I had proved myself the better man, 'Mo' was better known by sight to the thieves and 'sluggers' amongst whom we were about to adventure ourselves.

Behold me, then, on this sultry summer evening, sallying forth into the great world of London, concerning which I had heard so much, and of which knew so little. Out into the Strand we passed, and bent our steps first to the Coal Hole, one of the most famous of the 'song and supper rooms', as they were called, which, in those days, filled the place now occupied by the music halls. From there we went, I remember, to the Cyder Cellars, another similar resort, situated on the south side of Maiden Lane.

Both these places were filled to overflowing with well-dressed men and women, one or the other of whom contributed to the harmony of the evening every now and again, either voluntarily or at the request of the chairman. I was called on for a song, but, instead of complying, I borrowed a violin from one of the musicians and gave them my 'cuckoo solo', following this up by a medley of variations on some of the popular tunes of the day.

The applause, when I at length ceased, was terrific, and there were loud and persistent cries for an encore. So, for a change, I gave them an impromptu exhibition of what were then known as 'Grecian Statues', a very popular kind of show at that period, something like the modern living statuary, but with more drapery, and minus the white 'make-up'.

My giving this exhibition was a bit of vanity on my part, for I was proud of my form and figure, and the buzz of admiration that followed my first number, 'Hercules going forth to Battle', showed me that my pride was not altogether without justification. I was overwhelmed with congratulations at the finish, and many a bright eye looked invitingly into mine. But it was now near midnight, and the swells who were my employers were anxious to get on towards the Haymarket, so off we moved once more. The Haymarket, I should explain, was at this period the centre of attraction for young men bent on 'seeing life', and the scenes that were enacted there night after night are indescribable.

The street was like a fair. Every house on the left-hand side going up towards where is now Leicester Square was illuminated with Chinese lanterns. Oyster bars, supper-divans, song and dance rooms, 'gambling hells', and other even more questionable resorts abounded. The pavements were an ever-moving procession of gaily-dressed women, and men of all kinds and classes; while ranged all along the kerbs, each bent in out-vying the other in noise, were barrel-organ men, German bands, cornet-players, flautists, violinists; soloists, in fact, on every conceivable kind of instrument. Add to these, troupes of acrobats, 'peep-show' men, al fresco buskers of various sorts, who occupied nearly all the available space in the centre of the broad thoroughfare, and the reader can picture faintly the kind of place the Haymarket was fifty years back.

The 'fun' was at its height between two and three in the morning, for there was then no fixed hour for closing the public-houses, and these were consequently thronged from midnight till dawn, and often till long afterwards, with revellers and roysterers of both sexes, intermingled with pickpockets, garotters, bludgeon men, and other dangerous characters, the very scum of off-scourings of metropolitan rascaldom.

None of these pests, however, dared interfere with our party, for 'Mo' and I kept close to our charges, one on either side, and a look or a hint from either of us sufficed to warn off undesirables. The swells kept it up, though, till four in the morning, when they drove home, and left me free to return to Nat's, after one of the most tiring, albeit enjoyable, days I had spent in my lifetime.

Chapter 8
Matched to Fight Bill Thorpe

Nat Langham had not brought me to London, however, to act as bodyguard to his swell patrons at his house of entertainment. He believed I was destined to win battles in the ring, and looked to make money out of me, just as a racing man does who has discovered a promising yearling. He therefore kept me as 'dark' as possible, and I did little sparring, save at the semi-private exhibitions of the Rum-pum-pas, until the announcement was made that I had been matched to fight the famous Bill Thorpe for £50.

This was to be my first appearance in the London ring, and Nat and my other patrons and friends insisted on my going into strict training. This was an ordeal then very different from what it is now. Your modern boxer trains for a fortnight or three weeks, but in those days three months was considered none too much. Indeed, most of the really first-class trainers, men with a reputation to lose, would not consent to take over a man for a less period.

The methods in vogue too, at that period were far harsher and more drastic than they are at present. For instance, a favourite device, when a man had to take off much weight, was to cause him to run behind a dog-cart, holding on to the back, for ten, fifteen, or more miles, until he dropped through exhaustion, the ordeal being repeated day after day until sufficient adipose tissue had evaporated.

As, however, my weight was nearly normal at the start, and as I was, beside, in good condition, I was spared this particular infliction. Nevertheless, I found the proceedings sufficiently trying. From being a free agent, I suddenly found myself an absolute slave to an inexorable tyrant, whose word was law, and against whose decisions there was no appeal.

I had to go to bed when I was told, to get up when I was ordered, to eat and drink only what was allowed me, and that sparingly. My day began at dawn, where I took a warm bath, after which my trainer and his assistants took it in turns to rub me down vigorously with rough towels, finishing up with five minutes with the horsehair gloves, a proceeding which, at the beginning, used to make me smart all over, as if I had been beaten with stinging-nettles.

At nine I would start for my run, five miles out and five miles back, encased in double sweaters and wearing a woollen mask. This distance was gradually increased, until towards

Bill Thorpe, Mace's first opponent in the L.P.R.

the end of my training I could do my twenty miles a day at a jog trot without turning a hair.

Every evening my trainer would pickle my hands with a mixture of copperas, whisky, gunpowder, horseradish, and other ingredients, until by degrees they were made as hard as iron, and nearly as black. My face, too, was given a similar course of treatment, and with similar results. He was very anxious to treat my chest and ribs in like fashion, but against this one thing I protested successfully, for I was as vain as a girl of my torso. The result was that I presented a curious contrast when I at length entered the ring, my face and hands being well-nigh as black as a negro's, while the skin of my body was in sheen and colour like to old ivory.

The fight came off on February 17th, 1857, at a secluded spot near the mouth of the Medway. The day was a glorious one, more like a spring one in May, so that the swells were able to lie about at their ease on the grass of the outer ring, to obtain admission to which they had to pay a guinea each. This money did not, however, benefit us combatants, the whole of it going to the Pugilists' Benevolent Association.

Bill Thorpe was seconded by the redoubtable Tom Sayers and another pugilist whose name I cannot now recall. I had pinned my faith on a man named Bill Hayes and a Norwich friend of mine. The number of spectators was not very great, but it was select, the members of the Rum-pum-pas being, of course, there in force.

The wagering was consequently pretty heavy, a fact which Ould Nat took care I should not forget, his last words to me before I stepped into the ring being: 'Go in and win, my lad; remember, you are carrying not less than £2,000, bigger money than I have ever seen laid on a novice before'.

I needed no encouragement of the kind, however. I was fighting for my life, and I knew it. If I lost this, my first great fight, I could hardly hope to again secure the patronage necessary to enable me to meet a really first-class antagonist. 'Jem', I said to myself, as I faced my man, 'Jem, old boy, you *must* win'.

And so I did, after a battle which lasted twenty-seven minutes, during which time we fought seventeen rounds. It was not a very exciting fight, as prize-fights go, for I had my opponent mastered from the outset, and knew it. So for that reason I will not describe it at all minutely. I shall have some sufficiently exciting ones to tell about later on.

Suffice to say that after knocking him all over the ring, and administering much severe punishment, I gave him the *coup de grace* with a one, two, on the forehead and nose, so that he went to grass like a poled ox. He made an effort to rise when time was called, but immediately fell back again, and one of his seconds thereupon stepped to near the centre of the ring and threw his sponge in the air in token of surrender.

Mace thrashes Bill Thorpe

The fight, so eminently satisfactory to both myself and my backers, set the seal on my claim to be considered a coming man. I had no need now to go begging for patrons. Noble lords by the score, to say nothing of the lesser lights of the pugilistic world, were only too ready and willing to put their money down on my behalf. The only question was, who was to be my next antagonist?

Many meetings of my friends and patrons were held at Nat Langham's to settle this vital point, and at last it was arranged that I should do battle with a man named Mike Madden, a prize-fighter who, if not quite in the first flight, was known as a thoroughly game man, a tremendously powerful hitter, and a wary and skilful boxer. I was, of course, quite agreeable. In fact, I had to be, for a prize-fighter in those days was not the pampered pet he has since become. He was a paid gladiator, and as such it was his duty to do battle whenever he was told.

The stakes were to be £50 a side, as before, and these were duly deposited and articles signed. All went swimmingly, and I was looking forward with confidence to adding yet one more laurel to my wreath of victories, when all my hopes were dashed to the ground by a series of events which threatened for the time being to ruin my whole career.

Exactly what these events were I must leave until the next chapter to tell. It is a chapter I would willingly miss altogether, but when I come to think of it, I should like to tell the world, for the first and last time, how the two Madden fiascos really came about. I am an old man now. My race is nearly run. There is nothing to be gained by concealment, or by misrepresenting facts.

Only, as I said just now, I wish to begin with a new chapter. Suffice it to say here that my fight with Madden did not come off. Then I was then matched with him a second time. That fight again did not come off. That as a result all Britain cried shame on me, and called me a 'coward', the very boys in the street stopping to turn and jeer at me, while my Norfolk friends and backers were so frightfully incensed that they tried to burn down a house I had taken in Norwich.

It was all very terrible. From being the popular idol, I had fallen to be a by-word and a mockery.

It was not cowardice. No. A thousand times no. My after-career proved even to my enemies that that part of their charge, at all events, was quite unfounded.

Chapter 9
I Am Disgraced

As I related in my last chapter, immediately after my successful battle with Thorpe I was matched to fight one Mike Madden, a noted 'bruiser', and famous in prize-ring annals as the hero of the longest fight on record, a few minutes over seven hours. The stakes were £50 a side, and, as was usual at the time, the editor of *Bell's Life*, Mr. Frank Dowling, was entrusted with the duty of selecting a referee.

Upon this one circumstance there hinged all the trouble that followed. Mr. Dowling appointed to that responsible position a certain Dan Dismore. This man was obnoxious to my principal backer, Nat Langham, who had grave reasons, he said, for suspecting his straightforwardness. He accordingly, as soon as Dismore's name was mentioned, jumped into the ring and protested.

A heated argument ensued, Nat urging that for one thing Dismore had a lot of money on Madden, and was, therefore, almost certain to be prejudiced.

'Why', he exclaimed, 'you might just as well appoint me, who am known to be Mace's backer'.

Meanwhile, Madden and I had both stripped and were waiting to begin. The crowd around grew restless, and it looked as if there would be trouble.

Indeed, it seemed to me as if the ring was on the point of being rushed, when the tumult was temporarily put a stop to by Captain Barclay, a well-known sportsman, who strode forward and volunteered to take upon himself the duties of referee.

'At the same time, Mr. Langham', he said, turning to my backer, 'I think it only fair to tell you that I have myself backed Madden for a fiver'.

To this, Nat replied that he would be perfectly willing to accept the captain, even if he had fifty fivers on my opponent. 'I have every confidence in your fairness, sir', he concluded, 'while I have none whatever in Dismore's'.

With that Captain Barclay entered the ring and prepared to take up his duties. But at once there was a great outcry from Madden's supporters, a wild mob of Irishmen, hailing mostly from the purlieus of Drury Lane.

'Dismore! Dismore!' they shouted. 'We want Dismore or nobody. He is the officially appointed referee. If Langham refuses to allow Mace to fight under him, we claim forfeit'.

The famous prize-fighter, Mike Madden

'No! No!' screamed the other side. 'Barclay! Barclay! Let the captain officiate'.

From words, the mob quickly came to blows, as many as a dozen or more fights being soon in progress. The more respectable members of the crowd, becoming alarmed, beat a hasty retreat.

After this, pandemonium reigned. The shouting was frightful to hear.

'Get out of the ring', cried Madden to me, 'the fight is mine; you'll have to pay forfeit'.

'Perhaps I will', I answered, as savage as he, 'but it will be because of your trickery. And as for quitting the ring first, that will I not do, for I am not beaten'.

This question of precedence in leaving the ring may seem a small matter. But it was not so in reality, because according to the etiquette that governed prize-fighting in those days the loser in the battle always quitted the arena before his conqueror.

So there we stood glaring at one another, while the savage mob hurled all sorts of opprobrious epithets at the pair of us; the bulk of them, however, I am bound to say, being intended for me.

Eventually we both left the ring together, and the following day, as Nat and I had, of course, foreseen, the stakes were awarded to Madden.

Within twenty-four hours, however, a fresh match had been arranged. This was to have come off down the Thames, the rendezvous being London Bridge Station, and the time 6 a.m. But, as luck would have it, the night before my trainer caught me philandering about with a pretty little barmaid, who served in the tavern where we were staying on Holborn Hill.

He chided me for this, and rightly so, for by the unwritten law of the prize-ring, a man in training is forbidden to even look in the direction of a petticoat. But I, being young and hot-headed, took his well-meant rebuke in bad part, a violent quarrel ensued, and as a result he strode out of the place in anger, leaving me to my own devices.

What these were under the circumstances the reader may perhaps be able to guess. For almost the only time in my life, for I have always been an abstemious man, I took too much to drink. I retired late, or rather it was early in the morning. And when I awoke, the hour had long passed at which I should have put in an appearance at London Bridge.

My rage and mortification when I realised this knew no bounds. Out into the street I went, and again I had recourse to the cup that does sometimes cheer, but also invariably inebriates. Where I got to that day, or what I did, I could never recall properly. But my friends, who had been searching for me everywhere, found me late in the afternoon at a cricket-match in the

South of London. With me I had my bag of colours, and when I was discovered I was busily engaged in decorating with them the players on both sides.

Well, I had my fun, such as it was. I had vented my spleen. And now I had got to pay the penalty.

And very bitter that penalty was. I don't suppose that in the whole world of sport there were more than half-a-dozen men all told who had a good word to say for me. In Norwich, where I was formerly held in the highest esteem, the revulsion of feeling against me was so extreme that the mob attempted to burn down my house.

Mr. Frank Dowling, of *Bell's Life*, attacked me in language so severe that I shiver even now when I recall it. He dubbed me an 'arrant cur', and wrote of me in his editorial columns as 'the most unmitigated coward and impostor that ever laid claim to the title of a fighting man'.

In another part of his paper he pictured me as 'trembling all over like an aspen leaf, and as 'flying from the rendezvous like a stricken deer'. Finally he wound up as follows: 'Every patron of the ring is so disgusted at Mace's conduct that there is happily no chance of his ever again appearing in the fistic arena. Explanation on his part of the affair there can be none, so we advise him not to attempt it'.

He even went to the length of asserting that I had left secretly large sums of money in Norwich for the purpose of backing Madden. Although what good this would have done me, had I made up my mind to bolt, it is difficult to see, as under such circumstances all bets would, of course, have been off.

Even Nat Langham turned against me, although eventually he so far relented as to allow me to frequent on sufferance his boxing saloon at 'The Mitre', in St. Martin's Lane. Here I 'took on' with the gloves all comers, posing as 'an unknown', although, of course, the regular frequenters of the house knew me perfectly well. For an hour's hard boxing, just about this time, I have received as little as sixpence, and my remuneration seldom exceeded half-a-crown. From the gathering of the Rum-pum-pas, where gold was to be had, I was rigidly excluded.

Those were the blackest days of my life, and in secret I shed many bitter tears. Yet outwardly I showed a bold face, and kept telling myself that all would come right in the end. For, you see, I knew in my heart that I was no coward, as people were saying, but just a silly, hot-headed young man, who had gone and got drunk when he should have been attending to business, and who now bitterly regretted his folly.

Chapter 10
A Friend In Need

Matters went on thus for the better part of a year, and I had almost begun to despair, when one day there strolled into the saloon a tall, handsome man of aristocratic appearance. My heart gave a great jump, for I knew him at a glance. It was Lord Drumlanrig, he whom I had boxed with on that eventful evening, when, full of hope and bright anticipations, I had first come to London to seek my fortune.

As I said, I knew him at once, but he quite failed to recognise me, although, as it happened, I was at the time the only other occupant of the saloon. He looked round languidly, and he came over to where I was standing. 'I want a short bout with the gloves, my man', he said, 'will you oblige me?'

'Certainly, my lord', I replied, 'with pleasure', and at it we went.

I quickly found that there was something wrong with him. He boxed as cleverly as before, but more savagely, trying as it seemed to me to hurt me as much as possible by getting in vicious body blows, a manoeuvre hardly permissible in friendly bouts, such as ours was, although, of course, perfectly so in the ring.

For this reason I grew angry with him, and hit him hard about the head in return, so that for the second time when standing up to me his shirt was bloodstained. I did not know - how could I? - that he was even then standing on the brink of eternity, and that he himself was perfectly well aware of the fact.

I have thought since that it was his fate he was fighting, not me, for he went almost straight away from that encounter and took his own life.

Before leaving the saloon, however, he asked me who I was, and on my telling him, he remembered, and also that I was under a cloud. Turning to Nat, who had meanwhile entered the room, he said how cruel it was that a youngster like me should have his whole future blighted because of one foolish act.

'Whom', he asked, addressing me this time, 'would you like to fight?'

'Bob Brettle', I replied, flushing with pleasure and gratitude. (Brettle, I should explain, was at the time champion of the middleweights.)

'Well', he said, turning again to Nat, 'match him against Brettle, or any other man of his weight. You won't regret it, I promise you. If you don't care to do it for Mace's sake, do it for mine. It is the last favour I shall ever ask of you'.

Of course, this last phrase, which he spoke very slow and solemn like, puzzled the worried Nat not a little, for he could not understand what his lordship meant by it, any more than I could. We knew all too soon, though, as it turned out. And when the news came my heart sank within me, for I said to myself that now Lord Drumlanrig was dead, my chance of meeting Brettle was gone.

But Nat, although he said little had, I found out, made up his mind to keep the promise he had given. He would not, however, back me himself, or in my own name, even; but, working underground, he caused it to be announced that 'an unknown' had been found to fight Bob. Articles were signed, and in due course we met at the appointed rendezvous when great was the surprise of those who had come to witness the battle at finding that the 'unknown' was none other than myself.

Many, too, were angry and disappointed, and vented their spleen in sneers and unkind remarks. Foremost amongst these was Mr. Dowling, who remarked to me quite loud, so that everybody standing round could hear: 'What, do you mean to say you have dared to put in an appearance again?' Then, turning to a man named George Brown, who, acting under Nat's instructions, had made the match, he said: 'Why, George, do you mean to say that you have brought that cur out without a chain?'

My blood boiled at these repeated insults, but made no reply. Only all the way down - we travelled by steamer to the appointed place - I kept saying to myself, over and over again: 'Wait till the fighting begins; I'll show them then whether or not I am a coward'.

I never got the chance, however, for fate, as it turned out, was once more dead against me. We faced each other for barely three minutes, giving and receiving perhaps half a score of blows, when Brettle caught me a terrific left-hander on the point of the jaw, and down I went as if I had been poleaxed. It was a battle won by a fluke, as I proved conclusively later on by meeting and beating this same Bob Brettle in a battle royal which lasted over parts of two days. Nevertheless, my defeat did not add any lustre to my tarnished reputation, as may well be imagined.

It showed, however, that I was not exactly the poltroon I had been depicted, and I had now no great difficulty in getting backers. Amongst other fights for substantial stakes, from which I emerged victorious about this time, was one with 'Posh' Price, of Birmingham, whom I defeated in eleven rounds; also a fierce one with Travers, a negro, and one of the very gamest fighters I ever stood up to.

I was particularly anxious to meet and defeat Travers, as he had previously beaten the

Mace went down as if pole axed

famous Mike Madden, mentioned above, after a battle lasting ninety-seven minutes; and, of course, by prize-ring rules, my beating him would be equivalent to beating Mike. I had all my work cut out, though, and at one time it looked like my losing. The police broke up the fight on the first day, after six very heavy rounds, occupying twenty-one minutes. But on the day following the battle was resumed, and continued to a finish, Travers being compelled to give in after fighting fifty-seven rounds in seventy-one minutes.

It was during the autumn of the same year in which this battle was fought that I had my second encounter with Brettle, in which I proved victorious. This gave me what is known in prize-ring parlance as a 'clean record'. That is to say, that having beaten the only man who ever beat me, and having also defeated the man who had himself defeated the only man to whom I had ever had to pay forfeit, I was regarded as an unbeaten man myself, and eligible, therefore, to challenge for the Championship of England.

Chapter 11
I Fight Sam Hurst

This was held at the time by Sam Hurst, better known perhaps to fame as the 'Stalybridge Infant'. He was a perfect giant, standing over 6 ft 2 inches in height, and weighing nearly 17 stone.

As my height is only 5ft 9 inches and my average weight at that time did not exceed 10 stone 10Ib, it will be apparent that in challenging him, as I intended doing, I was conceding a great deal. Moreover, Hurst was a noted wrestler, the champion of Lancashire, in fact, and in those days wrestling played a by no means unimportant part in prize-fighting. His strength, too, was enormous, as poor Paddock, from whom he had wrested the championship, knew to his cost, one of the 'Infant's' sledgehammer blows having smashed in two of his ribs.

It was somewhat of an eye-opener, therefore, to the world of pugilism, when the announcement of the coming battle was first made public. Many of the 'knowing ones', indeed, professed the belief that it was only a 'blind', designed among other things to bring the custom of those interested to a sporting public-house which I then kept in the East End of London.

As a matter of fact, it did bring custom thereto, plenty of it, and of the right sort, so that the takings of the little house, with its one small bar, frequently exceeded £100 a night. I found, however, that life behind the beer-engines was not so conducive to 'keeping fit' as it might be; so I left the place in charge of an assistant, and accepted an offer to travel for six weeks with a circus at a guaranteed salary of £70 a week.

I was to give sparring exhibitions in the sawdust ring, and, of course, we took in Stalybridge. The scene there on the opening night was a sight to be remembered. From all parts of Cheshire and Lancashire special trains were run, and the people who crowded in to see me spar would have filled the great tent ten times over.

Their personal comments, when they did get in, were not flattering. 'What, that little whipper-snapper!' was a common remark. 'Im lick our Sam? Why, Sammy'll squash 'im like a cooked turnip'.

And such, indeed, seemed to be the general opinion, for the betting was all in favour of my antagonist, while both my friends and my enemies were for once agreed that this time, at

Sam Hurst, the 'Stalybridge Infant'

all events, I had 'bitten off more than I could chew'. The one notable exception was my old-time critic, Frank Dowling, who publicly retracted all that he had ever written regarding my alleged want of pluck, and also went out of his way to say that he should not be surprised to see me victorious – 'if', he added significantly, 'the fight is allowed to come off'.

Yes, this had now become the burning question. The prize ring was no longer what it used to be. The great Sayers-Heenan fight of the previous year had, by focusing public attention on the evils incidental to the sport, done much to strengthen the hands of the authorities, who were now openly announcing their intention of preventing all such exhibitions in future.

For this drastic action, the promoters of the battles fought about this time were largely to blame. Either carelessly or by design, the roughs were allowed free access to the places of meeting, with the result, of course, that the more respectable patrons of the ring were driven away.

It is true that some attempt was made to keep order and protect the peaceably inclined spectators from the depredations and violence of these human vermin. But such were not always successful. Indeed, it not infrequently happened that the special ring-keepers, who were appointed at a wage of a guinea a day by the Pugilists' Benevolent Association, were themselves overpowered, and in some cases badly beaten, by the ruffianly mob. As these ring-keepers were invariably trained boxers, specially selected for their strength and skill, it may be imagined what sort of chance the ordinary spectator would stand, did he venture to resent the loss of his property, or the ill-usage to which he was too often subjected.

It was resolved, however, both by my backers and by those who were championing Hurst, that on this occasion at all events, there should be no ruffianism if it could be possibly avoided. To this end, double the usual number of ring-keepers were engaged, while orders were given that no known rough characters were to be allowed to travel by the special train which was to convey us to the place selected for the fight, and this quite irrespective of whether they had managed to secure tickets or not.

None of these tickets, I should add, were sold until the night before the day upon which the event was to come off, and they could then be secured only from about half-a-dozen well-known patrons of the ring. Even the tickets told nothing to their purchasers, for neither station or time was indicated thereon. They were, in fact, simply vouchers, testifying that the holders had paid their money.

Ticket-holders were directed to assemble overnight in groups of so many, each group being told to go off to one of seven selected sporting houses. From these houses they drove in cabs, that had been previously chartered, to the appointed rendezvous, Fenchurch Street Station, where they were rapidly yet noiselessly entrained, just as the day was breaking.

By adopting these precautions both the police and the roughs were completely outwitted, the more so because the rumour had been industriously circulated that Paddington was to be the point of departure. Indeed, so well did this ruse work that the Great Western terminus was, we afterwards heard, besieged before dawn by crowds of undesirables, mingled amongst whom were scores of police and detectives, both in uniform and in plain clothes.

Meanwhile our 'special', bearing Hurst and myself, our backers, seconds, ring-keepers etc., and some four hundred selected spectators, was swiftly steaming through sleeping Essex, to roll anon into Southend just as the inhabitants of that now popular watering-place were beginning to arouse themselves for the day's occupation.

Naturally, the advent of our large party caused no little excitement. But the Southenders had barely time to rub their amazed eyes, still heavy with sleep, before we were off again. This time it was a small flotilla of tugs that bore us, on the broad bosom of Father Thames, across to the mouth of the Medway, up which we penetrated a little way, to disembark at last on a small island, all grass-covered and reed fringed, an ideal place for a fight. Not a soul was in sight, save ourselves. No house or other building was visible from our low-lying point of view. We were, for the time being, in a little world of our own.

The day was one of those perfect ones that come to us occasionally in mid-June; neither too hot nor too cold, a gentle breeze blowing, the sun shining gloriously from an opal-blue sky.

Quickly the ropes, stakes, and other paraphernalia were got out, and the business of pitching the rings began.

This took up some little time, for it had been previously arranged that the outer one should be pitched first, and that it should be made double the usual strength, by means of interlaced cords and special supporting stakes placed close together.

From this enclosure the keepers excluded everybody until the ring proper had been erected, when those who had their reserve tickets were admitted, but even these were kept a clear twelve feet away from the ropes wherein we were to fight.

By the time all these preliminaries were got through it was nearly nine o'clock, and it was precisely on the stroke of the hour when we entered the ring together. It was the first occasion upon which I beheld Hurst stripped for a fight, and I am free to confess that I was not altogether without misgivings as I ran my eye over my gigantic opponent's 'points'.

I can see him now as he stood there, the sunlight gleaming on his great muscles that bulged from his swarthy skin like bosses of beaten bronze. His broad, deep chest was covered with thick, matted hair, so that it more nearly resembled that of a gorilla than aught that was human.

There was, however, nothing else apelike about him, his carriage and figure being, so far as proportion went, models fit for a sculptor. His immense arms, brown and sinewy, were gnarled like to the branches of an oak tree, and his fists, black with prolonged pickling, were as big as cannon-balls and as rough and hard as two lumps of slag from a furnace.

I was all agog to be at him, being, in fact, for some reason or other, on this particular occasion as high-strung as a hysterical girl, so that the petty details of getting ready annoyed and irritated me as they had never done before. Yet not one of these formalities, so dear to the hearts of the seconds of those days, could be omitted.

First came the solemn casting into the ring of a kid-glove apiece, specially bought for the occasion, in token of the challenge, the said gloves becoming afterwards the perquisite of the principal ring-pitcher, one 'Puggy' White, who was wont to sell them to the highest bidder as a memento of the battle. Then followed the final touches to our toilets, these including, on this occasion, the anointing of my body with oil, in order to lessen the chance of the 'Infant' gripping me in his bear-like embrace.

Last, and most tedious formality of all, was the lacing of our fighting boots, a job which was rarely finished under the half-hour, and which frequently occupied much longer. These boots possessed some dozens of eyelet-holes, placed much closer together than those in a lady's stays. They were laced with cobbler's wax-end, and this was tightly fastened by a knot tied after each hole was traversed.

All things must come to an end at last, however, even the lacing up of a prize-fighter's boots, and presently 'Time' was called, and we advanced from our respective corners for round the first.

I had previously taken counsel with my seconds, and had received the advice, which I considered very good, to keep as much as possible out of his reach, trusting to my superior agility and quickness of delivery to overcome, in course of time, his superior strength and weight. Consequently, I found warily, getting in, however, two or three facers that marked him a bit, while I myself, at the end of the second round, was almost untouched.

In the second round Hurst came down with his spiked boot on my foot, lacerating it severely, and causing me excruciating pain. It was, of course, a pure accident, but a very nasty one none the less, and might easily have lost me the fight. But I had, by this time, pretty well gauged my antagonist, and felt sure that, barring accidents, I had him at my mercy.

Ding-dong we went at it. Or, rather, I should say, ding-dong I went at it, for his blows rarely reached me, while each one of mine went home, so that his face was soon in a shocking state. In vain he dashed at me like a mad bull, his huge nostrils dilated, his eyes, though half-closed from the effects of the punishment I had administered, blazing with passion.

He tried all he knew to get in one of his swinging body blows, like that which caved in poor Paddock's chest. But these tactics, as all boxers know, are fearfully dangerous, and again and again I got in over his guard.

By the end of the sixth round I had him beaten. He was nearly blind, covered in blood, and so badly winded that he could hardly stand up straight. My old antagonist, Bob Brettle, appealed to Hurst's seconds to throw up the sponge, and many of the spectators even, at the ringside, cried out for the fight to be stopped.

But Sam would not hear of it. Growling like an angry bear, the plucky fellow stood up for the seventh round, and again I was under the disagreeable necessity of administering punishment to an already vanquished foe. It was no use prolonging the agony, so I let him have it, smash, smash on his battered face.

Mace made a mess of Hurst's face

There were loud yells of 'Take him away!' and one of Hurst's seconds made as if to throw up the sponge. But Sam, and also some of his friends, objected, and he came up again to the scratch.

I did not know what to do, for the poor fellow was now quite blind, and kept tottering aimlessly about the ring. 'Look where he's going to, Jerry!' I called out to Jerry Noon, who was helping to second him. The giant heard my voice, and made a rush in the direction whence he supposed it to come from, his huge arms whirling like flails, his sightless and battered face working convulsively.

Of course, I easily avoided him, and, thinking to give him the *coup de grace*, landed him yet another left-hander between the eyes. He went down very heavily, but was up again for the next round, despite the protestations of the spectators and those of his own backers and seconds. Soon afterwards, however, another similar blow sent the game fellow to grass for the last time.

When 'Time' was called, he failed to respond, but lay there breathing stentorously, an inert, bloodstained figure, from which all knowledge and consciousness had temporarily vanished. Then the cheering broke out, long and loud, repeated yet again and again. I felt like joining in myself. For the ambition of my life was accomplished. I was Champion of England.

Chapter 12
Tom King's Challenge and Some Reminiscences

I was quickly made to realise that I was not to hold the title for long undisputed. Even while the noise of the cheering was yet ringing in my ears, there vaulted lightly into the bloodstained arena a lithe limbed young fellow, who stood confronting me.

'Yes?' I said inquiringly, although I guessed his errand.

For the answer he pulled a glove from the inner pocket of his jacket and threw it at my feet.

'Jem Mace', he cried, 'I am Tom King, and hereby challenge you to fight me for the championship belt you have just won. My backers have their money ready, and I am willing to meet you anywhere and at any time you please, the sooner the better'.

'Very well', I said, 'I will fight you'. And with that we shook hands, while the company crowded round and cheered more wildly than ever.

As soon as I had shaken hands with Tom King, after telling him how pleased I should be to fight him at the proper time and place, I turned to the crowd round the ring side, and, having borrowed a 'top' hat, which I held crown downwards in my right hand, addressed them something after this fashion:

'Gentlemen, there lies Sam Hurst, one of the gamest men that ever stepped into the ring. You have seen how bravely he fought today, and I want you to show your appreciation of him in a practical way. Gold will do if you haven't got silver, and I don't mind accepting banknotes if it so happens you haven't a sovereign handy. But mind, gents, no coppers, please. I want you all to give.

Those who have backed me will, I am sure, toe the scratch without being asked twice. While you who have backed Hurst ought to give also, for if you have lost your money, it has not been the fault of your man, who has fought for you pluckily and well'.

With that I passed round the hat, and the crowd, laughing good-humouredly, pressed forward with their offerings. These amounted in all to £35, which was not bad, considering all things.

We had just finished counting it out, when there was a loud shout from the outskirts of the

Mace collecting donations for Hurst

mob of onlookers. A detachment of police had put in a belated appearance, and we all, spectators and principals alike, had to take to our own heels to escape arrest. Poor Sam was driven off in a light cart that had been borrowed for the purpose, for he was quite unable to walk, let alone run.

It was, I reflected, a somewhat ignominious ending for what was to me one of the red-letter days of my life. But, then, there was no help for it.

On arriving at London I found, greatly to my alarm, that Hurst was still only semi-conscious. We drove him straight to his lodgings, and put him to bed, and for three days and nights I sat by him, not daring to leave his side, for we all thought he was going to die.

However, he presently rallied, and by the time fixed for the presentation to me of the stakes we had fought for (£400) he was able to be present at my little house in Holywell Lane, where the ceremony came off. It was a great night. Lots of well-known people were present, and the champagne flowed like water.

I shouldn't like to say how late, or rather early, it was before we broke up, partly because I don't exactly remember. But I know the sun was high in the heavens.

I got up a second subscription for him upon this occasion, which realised £15, making, with the money collected at the ring on the day of the battle, £50 altogether, not a bad solatium for a beaten prize-fighter in those days. Sam tried to return thanks, but could only mumble incoherently, on account of his lower jaw having been partially dislocated by one of my blows. He didn't so much mind not being able to speak, however, for, as he expressed it, he was never very good with the gab. What worried him was that he couldn't open his mouth wide enough to get the rim of a wine-glass properly into it, and so was missing his share of the 'fix'. We got over the difficulty presently, however, by inserting the long stem of a new church-warden pipe between his swollen lips, and filling the bowl with wine, which then, of course, flowed into his mouth and down his parched gullet in a continuous, and, no doubt, delightful, if somewhat meagre, stream.

Poor old Sam! As a fighter, I think he was one of the gamest, and at the same time, about the poorest, that ever gained championship honours. He won the belt from Paddock by a fluke, due to his colossal strength, which enabled him, as I have said, to smash in his opponent's ribs by means of a single lucky blow delivered with sledge-hammer force. But he was woefully deficient alike in science, in quickness of delivery, and in agility. Considered as a man, however, he was 'one of the best', generous, brave, and as simple as a child.

This latter quality caused some queer tricks to be played on him. I recollect, for instance, his coming to see a circus I was running some years later. After shaking hands with me and chatting over old times, I handed him free passes for the performance, as also for the various side-shows.

Amongst these latter was one conducted by a man named Holtum, who called himself the Cannon King, for the reason that one of his feats was the catching of a cannon-ball fired from a small cannon. The trick is not at all a difficult one if a man knows how to do it and is fairly strong, for, of course, the 'terrific' explosion inside the breech of the gun, like the flames and smoke belched from the muzzle, is for effect merely. The real motive power behind the ball is not gunpowder, but a spiral spring, which is released at the moment some loose powder (not rammed down, mind) is harmlessly burned inside the bore. Then out comes the ball, drops into the Cannon King's hands, and all is over, bar the applause, which is usually both long and loud.

At this time, and, indeed, for long afterwards, Holtum, taking a leaf from my book, offered £5 to anyone who could do the trick. But nobody tried, until simple Sam came along. He, urged by his friends, decided to have a go for it, and in due course he took his place in front of the cannon, feet firmly planted, hands outstretched ready for the catch.

Holtum, however, had no intention of letting him perform the feat, as may well be imagined.

So he ordered his attendant to decrease the tension of the spiral spring in such a way that, instead of sending the bell fairly high into the air at about the height of a man's head, it should eject it at a much lower level.

This was done. 'Are you ready?' was asked. 'Yes', shouted Sam valiantly. Bang went the gun. Out came the cannon-ball. But, needless to say, it was not caught by the 'Infant'. On the contrary, it caught him - right in the breadbasket - and he had a bread-basket then - and rolled him over like a dead snipe.

He was not, of course, seriously hurt. Holtum had carefully placed him too far away. But he was fearfully indignant, and wanted badly to fight the showman as soon as he had got his wind back. Hearing the commotion, I ran in, and, after a while, succeeded in quietening him. But I had a hard job.

'It's all very well for you to talk, Jem, old man', he kept saying, 'but you don't know what a buster it gave me. Why, you never hit me half so hard as that cannon-ball did'.

It was while I was running this self-same circus, by the way, that I started taking on all comers with the gloves, and offering a prize of £5 to anybody who succeeded in standing up before me for three three-minute rounds. John L. Sullivan and others have done this since, but at the time it was a bit of a novelty.

People wondered greatly at my temerity, and prophesied the loss of many 'fivers'. As a matter of fact, however, the offer was a perfectly safe one, as has been abundantly demonstrated during these latter years. No ordinary boxer can possibly stand up against a trained prize-fighter who has won his way to championship form for the length of time mentioned. Or, at all events, nobody ever succeeded in doing it with me.

One man, 'Tug' Wilson, managed to stay out the allotted time with John L. Sullivan, much to that champion's disgust. But then 'Tug' was a very clever boxer, indeed, a prize-fighter of the old school, and he adopted every device known to the expert in ring strategy in order to avoid punishment, going down as soon as he was touched, sparring for wind, ducking, feinting and so on. In this way he just managed to last out the specified number of rounds and win the prize, which in this case amounted to over £1,000. But it was not so much a boxing match as a carpet-crawling contest. I know, for I was there and saw it. Had 'Tug' stood up to John L. fair and square, he would have been knocked out in no time.

On some few occasions I have myself had to deal with these tricky gentlemen, but I always took good care to give them the upper-cut early in the first round, so as to make sure. Usually, however, my challengers, to do them justice, did not attempt any tactics of this shifty sort, but went straight for me, like a bull at a gate. Then, of course, the result was a foregone conclusion.

I would 'take a man's size', and if I thought it safe, would play with him up till half-way through the second round. But never longer. I wasn't taking any chances. I would not have minded so much losing a 'fiver', but I wasn't going to let it be said that an amateur had stood nine minutes before Jem Mace.

My favourite knock-out blow in these glove contests consisted in feinting with the right, and then landing with the left upon a spot called by old-time pugilists 'the mark' - about where the third button of the waistcoat falls. This generally did the trick. But, if it failed, a couple of left-handers in the throat would be pretty sure to finish the business.

Once, however, a chap managed to stand up until well into the third round, so that I began to get nervous. I forget his name, if ever I knew it, which is very doubtful. But he was a huge, brawny ironworker from the heart of the Black Country, and he visited my show while we were pitched at Bolton.

With him were thirty or forty of his mates, all black as niggers, and half-naked to boot, about as hard a looking crowd as it would be possible to conceive of. As soon as he got near enough to the circus to make himself heard, he roared out, 'Where's Mace?' in a voice that fairly made the canvas flap up and down with the vibration of it.

'Here I am', I replied, stepping out on to the front platform. 'What's the matter?'.

'Isn't it true tha'rt offering £5 to anybody as'll stand up to 'ee for three rounds?' was his next question.

'Quite true'.

'Well, I'm your man. I can stand twenty rounds'.

'All right', I said. 'Wait till the next performance. Then get to work, and if you succeed you get your money'.

And at the time appointed he did get to work, and that to such purpose that he very nearly got my money. He was, for all his great bulk, as agile as a cat, and as quick to strike as a rattlesnake. But that was not the worst of it. The man was as hard as a pebble. I hit him on the mark, over the heart, behind the ear, full on the jugular, gave him the benefit, in fact, of all the most deadly blows known to pugilists. Yet he came up smiling every time. I even hit him so hard once on the forehead that I burst one of the nearly new boxing gloves to pieces, and all boxers know how difficult - well-nigh impossible, in fact - a feat this is.

In the end, however, he had to give in, but if he had been able to have held out for another thirty seconds or so the 'fiver' would have been his. So struck was I with the man's gameness that I gave him a sovereign to drink my health, whereupon he and his following struck up 'For he's a jolly good fellow', and sang it with such lusty energy and strength of lung that it was heard, I was afterwards informed, at a distance of over two miles.

Of course, being Champion of England brought me a good deal of attention, and made my name very prominent in certain circles. Indeed, I am afraid I was in the way of getting spoiled, when an incident occurred which pulled me down a peg or two by showing me that fame such as mine was, after all, largely a matter of latitude and longitude.

It came about in this way. A gentleman who had heard of the Grecian statue performances of my earlier days thought it would prove a drawing card if he got me to give a series of these exhibitions at different places. He offered me a good round sum for a run of forty-two nights, money down in advance, and as I happened to be doing nothing in particular just then I concluded to take it on.

We opened in Wigan to a crowded house, and then struck south, giving one evening performance at each town we stopped in. The itinerary, however, had been badly arranged. Amongst the places we visited were several small country towns, some scarcely more than villages, in fact, and whose inhabitants took apparently little or no interest in sport.

As a result, the receipts dwindled alarmingly. This did not, of course, matter greatly to me. I had my money all right. But the face of my manager grew glummer and glummer. At last one night the climax was reached. We were at a show at a certain place in the Midlands, and at the appointed hour we had an audience of one only.

That was all. The 'great Jem Mace, champion pugilist of the world', as I was styled on the bills, had been brought all the way from London to be gazed upon by a solitary individual. And even he, I discovered later, had not paid for his ticket.

Next day we 'chucked' the rest of the tour, and returned to town, where I gave the remainder of the performances contracted for in various East End and suburban halls. We did better at these, but I do not think the man who invested his money on the strength of my name succeeded in recouping himself. In fact, I know he did not. And, in a sense, it served him right, for had he taken my advice as regards the choice of towns, the result, I have no reason to doubt, would have been quite different.

It was about this time that I first became acquainted with the famous Adah Isaacs Menken, and, of course, I fell under the spell of her beauty and witchery, as indeed did all men upon whom she chose to exercise them.

The wayward Adah was then the wife of John Heenan, who fought the great battle with Tom Sayers for the championship at Farnborough, on April 17th, 1860. I have met many women in my time, pretty and otherwise, good women and bad women, clever women, too; but never did I come across one who could hold a candle to this peerless creature.

Her physical beauty alone, both of face and form, was superb, so that when she appeared at Astley's Amphitheatre as 'Mazeppa', all London flocked to see her, and her share of the takings amounted to £200 a week for many months together. But it was her remarkable cleverness, and the quickness of her perception, which I think, mostly drew men to her; else how would she have captured, as she did, such geniuses as Dickens, Reade, and Swinburne, to say nothing of the elder Dumas and Theophile Gautier?

Actress, poet, sculptor, painter, and many things beside, her life was a varied and wonderful one. Before she was fourteen her singing and dancing had taken New Orleans by storm. At seventeen she had been wed and deserted. Altogether she was married four and divorced three times.

When I knew her she would be about twenty-eight or twenty-nine years old, and for a time I thought she seemed to favour me greatly. But I presently discovered that it was really my partner and cousin, Pooley Mace, whom she was after, for which I was not altogether unthankful. Life as Adah's acknowledged lover would have been too exciting just then to have been altogether to my liking.

Poor girl! Little did I imagine, as I saw her, radiant in her youthful beauty, dispensing hospitality to her chosen intimates at the Saturday-night supper-parties she was so fond of giving, that within three or four short years she would be lying dead in an alien land. Yet so it was. She caught a chill while rehearsing in Paris, and expired there in August 1868. Whenever business or pleasure takes me to the French capital, I always pay a visit to her tomb. It is in the beautiful Pere la Chaise cemetery, and bears the simple inscription, chosen, I believe, by herself, 'Thou Knowest'.

But these reminiscences are by the way, although I hope they will interest the reader in the perusal as greatly as they do me in recalling them. What I want to tell about chiefly, however, just now, is my first fight with Tom King.

Chapter 13
I Fight Tom King

He was a brave man, was Tom, and a fine fighter. He first made his name when working at the London docks, unloading guano ships, a most unsavoury occupation, besides being so laborious that none but the very strongest men were able to stand it.

Tom was a sort of a stevedore, or petty foreman in charge of a gang, and under him were some pretty tough characters. One of these, called the Terror of Wapping, fell foul of Tom, and received a tremendous hiding for his pains. The 'mill' got talked about, for it was, by all accounts, a very prolonged and stubborn one, in which a lot of gameness and science was shown on both sides; and eventually the news reached the ears of Jem Ward, the old ex-champion, who at the time kept a public-house in East London.

Now Jem was always on the lookout for 'dark horses' amongst the fighting fraternity, by backing whom, if his judgement was sound, he could make no end of money. So off he went to

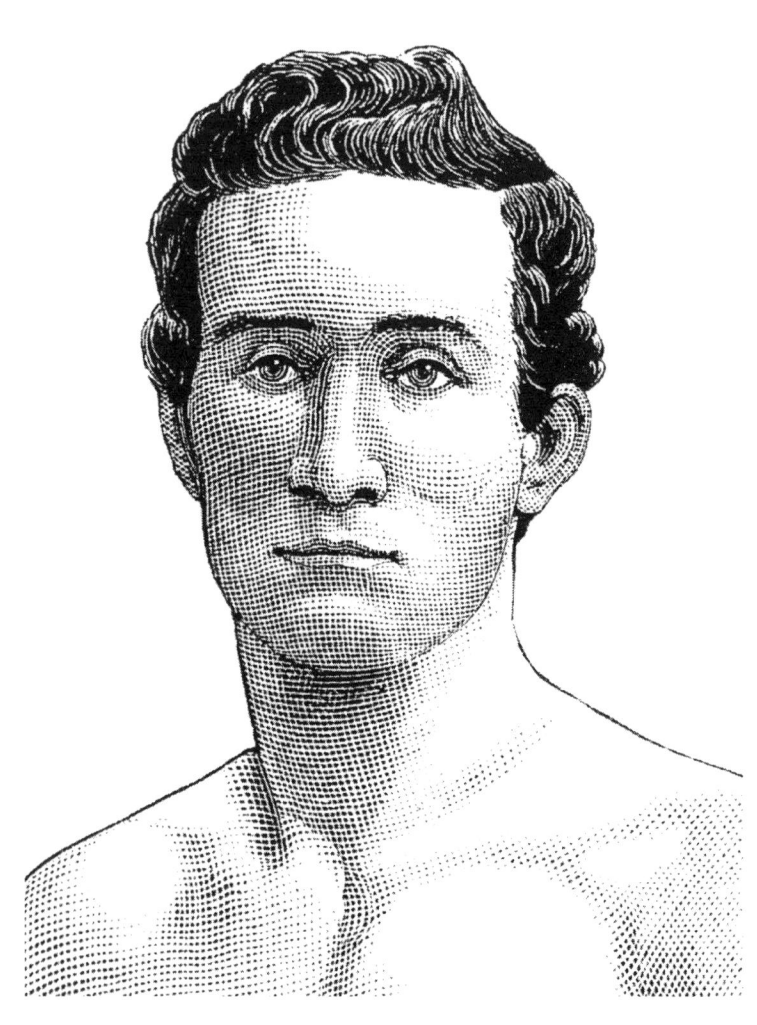

Tom King, hero of London's East-end

Wapping to seek Tom, and having found him he got him to put on the gloves with some of his old customers, men he could trust.

Ward has often told me since what an eye-opener to them all was Tom's style of fighting, and how he (Ward) made up his mind at once to match him against me. I was just then, however, backed to fight Sam Hurst, so Tom had to wait his turn. Meanwhile he met and defeated two noted bruisers named Truckle and Broome, winning fame and some money for himself and for his backer, the astute Jem Ward, some hundreds of pounds in bets.

As the last of these two battles came off in the interval between King's challenging me for the championship and our meeting to fight for it, naturally I went to see it, for, of course, I was anxious to know from the evidence of my own eyes how Tom shaped in the ring.

It was a pretty fight, and Tom was, I will say, a very pretty fellow. Standing well over 6 ft. 2 inches in height, and weighing between 13 and 14 stone, he was a veritable giant in point of size. Yet for all his weight and bigness he looked hard and fit. 'Jem', I said to myself, 'I think he will prove a hard nut for you to crack.'

I didn't *think* it though, after the battle was finished; I *knew* it. I never saw a big man fight so fast or so fiercely as did Tom King during this encounter of his with Broome. Talk about greased lightning! His fists shot out right and left, time and time again, quicker than the eye could follow. In forty-five minutes by the clock he had his antagonist knocked out, and I was one of the first to shake him by the hand and offer congratulations. Then I toddled off to the station all by myself, deep in thought. The very next day I went into strict training. It wouldn't do, I could see, to take any chances with a pugilist of Tom's calibre.

The morning of the day on which I was to meet him – it was mid January – dawned cold and cheerless. In fact the weather all through was of the most atrocious description, rain falling in torrents without a moment's intermission. Nevertheless there was a fairly big gathering at the ring, which was pitched at Godstone, in Surrey.

Both of us, I remember, started shivering violently as soon as our warm flannels were removed; and no wonder, for the bitter wind drove the ice-cold rain against our bare bodies with punishing violence, numbing us, and yet at the same time stinging us like so many whip-ends. The result was that, instead of fighting, we both started rubbing our chests and arms, in order to try and restore, if possible, the suddenly suspended circulation.

I suppose it looked rather ludicrous to the spectators, for some jeered and more laughed, while one or two would-be wits inquired with mock anxiety whether we had brought our powder-puffs with us. These taunts, and others far coarser, seemed to rile Tom, for he suddenly cried out, 'Are you ready, Jem?'

'Quite', I replied. And with that we went at it.

I very soon found that I had not under-rated my antagonist's ability. He was not, although I say it, my match in ring-craft, but he had the advantage of me in weight and height, besides being five years younger, and I knew I should have to put forth my very best to beat him.

Notwithstanding my 'best', however, he got in at me first, landing me a smashing left-hander on the mouth, cutting it badly and filling it with blood. It was a painful blow, but in a sense it was a lucky one for me. It told me, in language I could hardly fail to understand, to be careful.

All my care, however, did not prevent so clever and quick a hitter from getting home on me again and again. By the end of the twenty-second round my left eye was entirely closed, and my mouth was knocked all out of shape, while Tom was marked scarcely at all.

But this was because, while he had been pounding my face, I had been hitting his body. Again and again I struck him on the mark, and I had thrice got in a heavy right-hander over the heart. This sort of punishment, I reflected, must tell in the long run.

The question was, though, was I going to be blinded first, or Tom winded, for he had got in a terrific smash on my up-to-now undamaged eye, causing it to swell alarmingly. If I lost the sight of my right, as I had already done that of my left, I was done for.

Meanwhile the pitiless rain was pouring down on us unceasingly, converting the ring into a quagmire, which our feet churned into a pasty, sticky mess. It interfered seriously with my fighting capabilities, and probably also with King's, for we could get no foothold, frequently slipping and slithering in all directions.

It was to this that I attribute the receipt of the crushing blow which Tom managed to get in towards the end of the twenty-seventh round. I meant to have closed in under his guard, with the object of seizing and throwing him, thinking to wind him more. But as I ducked I also slipped, and he, quick as lightning to seize the opportunity, struck up from beneath at my face, knocking me clean off my pins and well-nigh head over heels.

I thought my neck was broken, and no wonder, for I had pitched with all my weight on the back of my head. Lucky for me, just then, that the ground inside the ring was of the consistency of pease-pudding.

The blow, moreover, had still further damaged my only available eye, so that I could only just see through a slit. This, though, was remedied in the next round, and by my antagonist, who struck me a glancing blow with his knuckles, gashing severely the overhanging lump of flesh that was obstructing my sight.

This had the effect of causing the blood to flow abundantly, thereby reducing the swelling.

And now, at last, the tide begins to turn in my favour. My long succession of body blows are commencing to do their work. As he sits on his second's knees between the rounds I can see his mighty chest painfully expanding and contracting, and hear the short, sharp gasps, almost like sobs, that tell of 'bellows to mend'.

At it again! Surely it *can't* last *much* longer! In the thirtieth round I did what I attempted to do in the twenty-seventh, I gripped him, that is to say, put on the back-heel, and dropped him heavily on his head and shoulders. 'Bravo, Mace!' yelled the crowd. 'Stick to him', advised my seconds. 'Give him no rest. Body blows and back falls, mind, are going to win you the fight'.

This was excellent advice, and exactly coincided with my own views. So, as you may well imagine, I was not slow to act upon it. I threw him again and again, dashing him violently to the ground, and frequently falling on him, so that I thought more than once that all the breath must certainly be knocked out of his body. But, no! He came up smiling again each time, and things began to look serious. I was, I felt, getting weaker, and my eye was again beginning to swell. Was I to lose the battle after all? Evidently the spectators did not think so, for in the lulls of the fighting I could hear them shouting the odds on me; heavy odds, too, and no takers. 'Mace! Mace!' they kept screaming out. 'Mace is sure to win!' But I myself was not so sure.

More especially was this so after the thirty-second round, when King, copying my earlier tactics, hit me a terrible punishing body blow. It was one of those swinging, sledge-hammer punches, such as big, powerful men of King's type can administer at times with frightful effect. It caught me in the side, just under the left armpit, and at the time I thought my chest was smashed in. 'Oh, Jack', I whispered groaningly to my chief second, Jack Hicks, as he led me to my corner. 'I am in pain'.

'In pain? Of course you're in pain', was his somewhat unsympathetic reply. 'But what about Tom? You don't suppose he feels exactly comfortable, do you?

No, I didn't suppose that, of course. And if I did I should only have had to have looked him over once to have been undeceived.

Poor Tom. What a sight he was to be sure. His once handsome face was by this time all cut and disfigured. But best sign of all, from my point of view, were the broad red blotches, each the bigness of a baby's head that mottled the white skin of his chest and ribs all over like the crimson blobs on a child's toy rocking-horse.

It was not, however, until he stood up for the forty-second round that I knew for certain the end had come. The wild rush he made at me

King though damaged, was still as game as ever

told me so. I have learned to know both that look and that rush.

So I dodged his mad rush, and played him about the ring until I saw his lower jaw begin to drop from sheer exhaustion. Then I sprang at him, and, summoning every ounce of strength I had left, dealt him a smashing blow on the throat. He would have fallen with that. But I took care he should do nothing of the kind. Not that I did not want him to fall. Only not that way.

I wanted him to fall my way, and he did. For immediately following the throat blow, I gripped him round the body, got what wrestlers call the 'crook' on him, turned him half round, and dashed him face forwards to the ground, myself falling on top of him.

That finished him. There was no more stir nor life in him than in a bale of wool. 'Time' was called, and then 'Time' again. But Tom did not move. The referee, watch in hand, entered the ring, and counted off the customary eight seconds grace. Then, as there was no response from King's corner, he turned to me and said, 'Mace, you have won the fight; I congratulate you'.

At this there was a general cry of 'the better man has won', an opinion in which, needless to say, I thoroughly concurred. There was, however, one man who thought differently, and that was Tom King himself, as the reader will presently see.

Chapter 14
My Second Fight with Tom King

King professed to be by no means satisfied at the result of his first battle with me, and insisted over and over again that he could have beaten me had he not been wrongly advised by his seconds, who urged him, against his better judgement, to force the pace in the earlier stages of the encounter.

Of course, I had no choice but to fight him again, if he so desired. But I pointed out to him that there was no hurry, and to this he agreed, the more readily as Mr. Ginnett had come forward and offered a joint engagement for six months at his circus on what we both considered very liberal terms indeed.

So a few weeks after the close of the contest we started to tour the provinces, giving sparring exhibitions that drew enormous crowds.

Those six months were, I think, about the pleasantest I ever spent. I had practically nothing to do, for after the hard knockabout work I had been accustomed to, the few playful rounds I sparred with Tom each day counted for very little. The money came rolling in, for the big circus tent was crammed at every performance, and our share of the takings seldom fell below £50 a week apiece, and was often a great deal more. We travelled first-class, put up at the best hotels, and generally 'did ourselves well'.

Meanwhile Tom and I, thrown closely together as we were, became the fastest of friends, and I could not help thinking what a pity it was that we must shortly start to batter one another about again. He, however, as perhaps was only natural, did not look at the matter from quite the same standpoint, as the following incident will show.

The spring was well advanced, and we had settled between ourselves that the battle should come off in the early autumn, when there appeared in *Bell's Life*, to Tom's utter astonishment and dismay, a challenge from an 'Unknown' to fight me for the championship and £200 a side. At first we both thought it was a joke. But on hurrying to the office of the newspaper in question I was informed that the challenge was a genuine one, that it was in perfect order, and that, moreover, the sum of £20 had been staked as earnest money.

This, in my hurry and confusion, I covered; only to find out afterwards that I need not have done so, as my prior engagement with King, although informal, barred all other aspirants for the time being. The net result was that I lost my money to the mysterious 'Unknown', for, of course, he took it when I forfeited, and both Tom and I - Tom especially - were made to suffer considerable inconvenience and suspense while the matter was under consideration by the committee of the prize ring.

After this, to clinch matters, we signed formal articles, the battle being fixed therein to come off in November. Tom, who had been on thorns all the while lest he should be diddled out of meeting me owing to the curious *contretemps* alluded to above, heaved quite a sigh of relief as he affixed his signature; we both went into training, he at the 'Bald-faced Stag', Woodford, then a remote and little visited wayside inn, while I journeyed to Newmarket, where I took over Tom Sayers' old quarters. At the last moment, however, there was another hitch. The South-Western Railway Company, after having first agreed to provide a special train to take us and our friends and backers to the place of meeting, cried off at the last moment, in obedience to the clamour of a certain section of the Press.

Here was a pretty go. Lots of people had paid their two guineas for tickets. The sporting public-houses were filled overnight with would-be spectators. Tom and I were ready and willing. Yet it seemed, nevertheless, that the whole affair was going to end in smoke. King, I was told, shed tears of mortification when the news was told to him. As for me, I was, I must confess, more philosophical. You see, I had money to lose, and not nearly so much to gain, for was I not already Champion of England?

Nevertheless, I cannot say that I was exactly sorry when it was whispered to me about midnight that a fresh rendezvous had been arranged. This was Fenchurch Street Station, whence we were to travel by ordinary train to a spot that was to be indicated later on in the day.

Four o'clock a.m. was the hour named, and we were warned to be there early 'For', as one of my seconds remarked, 'there's going to be a pretty rough crowd there'. I knew what that meant, so, taking time by the forelock, I drove up to the station a little before three. Even then, however, the roughs were commencing to gather.

How they got the tip, or whence they came, no one seemed to know. But there they were in their hundreds, I had almost said in their thousands - a savage, ugly mob, bent on mischief.

The swells who drove up in cabs fared the worst. Some fought their way through to the platform and comparative safety. But many more were driven back, after having been robbed of all they possessed, and beaten into the bargain. The few police about declined to interfere, on the grounds that we ourselves were about to engage in an illegal action. The stewards did what they could, but that was not a great deal.

Still, the crowd of roughs did not have it entirely their way. Practically all the intending spectators, and the others interested in the approaching battle, were strong men in the prime of life, able and willing to use their fists. Old Bill Richardson, of the 'Blue Anchor' public-house, an enormously powerful man, and a famous sportsman of his day and generation, fought his way through the howling mob, I remember, with the aid of the butt end of a broken billiard-cue. Bob Travers, my old antagonist, brought a couple of knuckle-dusters into play, one on either hand. Nevertheless, he was badly mauled, besides losing a valuable gold watch and chain.

For this disgraceful rowdyism, I consider the authorities were principally to blame. That we were going to do something that was nominally illegal, namely engage in a prize-fight, was perfectly true. But I did not think then, and I do not consider now, that the police were, therefore, justified in allowing us to be mobbed well-nigh to death by a collection of the most dangerous ruffians in London. They might have found some other way of punishing us after committing the offence, and prevented the rabble from cracking our skulls in advance.

This, however, is by the way. Nor did we trouble very much about it at the time. Those who meant getting through mostly managed to do so, sooner or later, and by seven o'clock we were 'all aboard', and on our way to Thames Haven. Here we found a couple of steamers, chartered overnight, in waiting to take us up 'the little river', as pugilists in those days termed the Medway. The sight of the peaceful countryside, however, with a sweet little piece of lawn-like turf at the back of an old barn - 'just the place for a mill', as one enthusiast put it - proved irresistible. 'Why not fight it out here?' asked Tom. 'Why not?' I asked in return. The principal backers nodded to one another. The ring-keepers hurried forward with the ropes and stakes, and almost before one could say 'Jack Robinson' the arena was ready.

As before, King forced the fighting from the first, a thing I had not expected after what he had said after being beaten through adopting these very tactics. Again, too, he drew first blood with a smashing blow to the mouth, a mishap that was largely due to my attention being distracted by a row in the outer ring, where some of the roughs were being chastised by the ring-keepers for attempting to force their way into the inner enclosure. I only gave one flashing glance in their direction, but Tom was quick to take advantage of it. And after that I kept my eyes on my antagonist, and left the crowd to look after itself.

Somehow, I felt sure of winning that fight. And the spectators seemed to share my opinion, for the betting was all in my favour, as much as 20 to 1 being offered, and no takers. However, after we had been fighting for about five minutes or so, Tom cross-buttocked me, and gave me one of the nastiest falls I ever had in my life. I landed upside down on top of my head, and everybody thought my neck was broken.

As luck would have it, however, I was not much hurt, nor even greatly shaken, incredible though it may sound. I jumped to my feet in an instant, and called out in answer to a hundred anxious enquiries: 'I'm all right. You'll see the next round'.

And they did see, for from that instant I seemed to have it all my own way. Tom tried all he knew, varying his tactics almost with every round. At one moment he would be leaping straight at me like a panther, the next he would be dancing round and round me like a cat on hot bricks. But all the while I kept on pounding him, and with each round I could see his strength getting less and less.

At length came the time when I thought I might safely sail in and finish him. He was nearly blind, his head was double its normal size, and he reeled like a drunken man whenever he attempted, to stand still for even the fraction of a second. The shouting and uproar round the ring were frightful, but above all the babel of sound I could hear the stentorian voice of Johnny Gideon - 'The

Rothschild of the Ring' they called him - offering to lay '£100 to £1 on Mace'.

And then! Well, how it happened I do not properly know even now. I remember walking warily up to the tottering, bleeding, half-blind figure that shared the ring with me. I recollect saying to myself that I must be careful and not hit my old pal too hard, because he was already a beaten man. The next instant I had trodden on a bit of turf that was slippery with blood, and felt myself falling - falling.

I tried to recover my balance, and had partly succeeded, when - smash! Tom had landed me one of those tremendous swinging round-arm blows on the side of the jaw, rolling me head over heels like a shot rabbit. I was told afterwards that it sounded more like a kick from a horse's hoof than a blow from a human fist, and I can quite believe it.

They carried me to my corner and my seconds tried all the familiar tricks to bring me round, biting my ears, tickling my throat with a feather, and so on. By these means I was enabled to toe the scratch twice more. But it was all to no purpose. That one blow of King's had made him Champion of England.

I can see him now as I stagger towards him and he makes up as if to strike me. Then, seeing I can no more defend myself than could an infant in arms, he whispers softly: 'Jem, old man, chuck it, you're done for'.

Of course I shake my head but very feebly. Whereupon he walks up to me and pushes me over, but half-holding me up, too, at the same time, so that I shall not fall too hardly, just as one does when romping with a child. Twice is this repeated. Then I lapse into merciful unconsciousness.

So I lose the championship - by a fluke! Yesterday I was, in certain circles, the most sought-after man in England. I could, and did, earn from £50 to £100 a week, merely by exhibiting myself. Tomorrow I should be unable, as I well knew, to earn as many shillings. The world had no use in those days for a beaten prize fighter. Could anything be more vexatious?

All night I lay awake. My face was swollen in the most alarming manner, and I suffered great pain. But the physical agony I underwent was as nothing to the mental. To think that victory had been snatched from me at the moment it seemed, nay, actually was, in my grasp, and by an accident. It was too cruel.

Chapter 15
Tom King Retires

I found comfort, however, in the reflection that Tom was now Champion of England. He was bound, in consequence, to meet all-comers, myself included, or forfeit the belt. I had only to challenge him again.

But supposing somebody else challenged him first? I might then have to wait in obscurity for the better part of a year. Horror! The thing was unthinkable. I jump out of bed in a trice. It is barely six and yet dark, but I hastily dress in candle-light, and after partaking of a scratch breakfast of 'spoon victuals' hurry westwards, my objective being, of course, the office of *Bell's Life*.

'No', I am informed, 'nobody had been there before me'. I heave a sigh of relief, and wait as patiently as I can until the editor, Mr. Dowling, puts in an appearance. Promptly on his arrival I explain my errand, at the same time planking down my earnest money. 'Very well, Mace', says Mr. D., 'I will see that your challenge is made public. Meanwhile, you are secure. King will have to meet you again or surrender the belt'.

With that we shake hands all round, champagne is uncorked, and we pledge one another in goodly bumpers. Then, almost before I know where I am, one of the staff takes me by the arm, and hurries me through a passage into what printers call the 'composing room'. Naturally, the men all look up from their work wonderingly, while I, having an inkling of what is coming, try to turn tail.

Before I can get back to the doorway, I however, am forced rightabout, while a voice bawls out, 'Gentlemen, allow me to introduce you to the "coward".

For a single instant they hardly appeared to understand. There was a pause. A low murmur of puzzled bewilderment. But then the cheering broke out, loud and long, continuing for several minutes. I don't think I ever had such another reception anywhere, so spontaneous and so hearty. They crowded round, and nearly shook my arms out of their sockets. How they yelled, to be sure! Some danced about the room, as though they were temporarily bereft of their senses. Finally one man, in an excess of enthusiasm, seized hold of his tray of type and hurled it into the air, the little leaden letters falling in a shower all round us.

'Well', I said to myself as I took my leave, 'if I am beaten I am not disgraced, nor have I apparently lost a great deal of my popularity'.

But a week passed by, two weeks, a month, and Tom showed no disposition to accept my challenge. I was told that he was going to be married, and had definitely made up his mind to retire from the ring. He would fight no more.

Naturally, this was very disappointing news to me. Of course, if he adhered to his determination, the belt would come back to me in due course, and without my having to do battle for it. But this was not what I wanted. I wanted to fight out the rubber, and win it, as I was confident I should do.

I tried every way I could think of to induce him to alter his decision. I even offered him £100 if he would meet me. This was on the stage of what was then known as Weston's Music Hall, in Holborn, the house that was afterwards called the Royal, and is now the Holborn Empire. Finally, losing all patience, and acting on a sudden uncontrollable impulse, I struck him lightly on the face with my open hand one morning when we chanced to meet, quite accidentally, outside Tattersall's.

Naturally, Tom wasn't going to stand that sort of thing. He hit back, and in the twinkling of an eye we were all over one another.

I don't suppose that two champion pugilists ever before performed to so small an audience. A score or so of loungers, half-a-dozen small boys and a couple of slatternly women made up the sum total.

However, I have no doubt that the crowd would have been very quickly reinforced as regards numbers, had we been permitted to continue our impromptu mill. But we were not. Hardly had we begun to warm to our work, when up strolled the inevitable policeman.

'Now then, you chaps', he cried, 'just stop that and clear, or I'll fight the pair of you myself.

This remark quite upset Tom's gravity, as it did also mine, so that we laughed long and heartily.

'Wot're yer larfin at?' asked the man in blue, evidently displeased. 'D'ye think I couldn't do it?"

Well', said Tom, 'I don't know about *fighting* us, but do you think you could *beat* us?'

'Do I *think* I could?' reiterated the policeman. 'Do I *know* I could? That's the question. Why, man' - this with great impressiveness - 'I'm the champion boxer of my division'.

'Oh, you are, are you?' replied Tom. 'Well, allow me to inform you that *I'm* the champion of *England*'.

'And allow *me* to inform you', retorted the bobby with some heat, 'that you are a liar. Tom King is champion of England. I know him well, and you're not a bit like him. *Why, you might as well try and stuff into me that your blackguardly looking pal here is Jem Mace.* Be off, the pair of you, or I'll have you locked up; and then you can tell the 'beak' in the morning what your *real* names are. I warrant they are well enough known at Bow Street'.

As he looked as though he meant what he said, and as by this time the street was full of people, we took his advice. But he followed us a few yards in rear, to see us clear off his beat, and all the while we could hear him muttering: 'Tom King, indeed! Jem Mace! Humph! The cheek of it! A couple of lazy loafers! I don't suppose either of 'em can box for nuts'.

This was almost my last meeting with King, except casually, for he kept his word, so far as I was concerned, and resolutely refused to fight. He did, however, consent some time later to meet Heenan, being tempted by the up till then unprecedentedly large purse of £2,000. Afterwards he became a bookmaker, and died very well off indeed, his will being sworn, unless my memory deceives me, at something over £50,000.

Meanwhile, I was placed in a somewhat awkward position. I was not champion, but the challenger of the champion, and the champion would not respond. I could only bide my time, and this I did at the little hostelry which, as I have previously mentioned, I owned in Holywell Lane, Shoreditch. Here, evening after evening, my old friends and patrons gathered round me, and we had some merry times.

We were a sporting lot, and many were the strange wagers that we made in that cosy bar parlour. One I particularly call to mind, because it had to do with my house. I used to display in the front window a pair of huge carvers, which no man would have dreamt of putting to their proper use, unless indeed he had an entire carcase to deal with.

I had taken them over with the lease of the premises from the former proprietor, a man named 'Spider' Hoiles, and the story attached to them was that by their aid his (the 'Spider's') predecessor had once killed, skinned, cooked, carved, and eaten a whole sheep in three days. On the night I have in mind this astronomical feat became the subject of general conversation, some holding that it was quite possible, even easy, of accomplishment, while others took the opposite view.

In the end, after much argument, a certain Jack Howard, an old trainer of mine, said that he would undertake to find a man who would repeat the experiment, and backed his assertion with a ten-pound note. This was instantly covered. Many other side-bets were made, until by the time the first day of the trial arrived I suppose there must have been between £200 and £300 depending upon the result.

Howard's champion sheep-eater proved to be a lanky woolcomber from Bradford, who looked as if he had not enjoyed a good meal for months. He evidently understood something of butchering, however, for he killed the sheep we had provided in a trice, afterwards skinning it in a most masterly manner.

Next he proceeded to roast it whole in an oven, kindly lent for the purpose by a sporting baker who lived nearby, and as soon as it was done he set to work on it with the big carvers. At the beginning he made capital progress, eating a whole leg for dinner, and the best part of a shoulder for supper. But after that there came a woeful falling off, and by the end of the allotted time he had not succeeded in consuming much more than half a carcase. He went away very crestfallen, for he had been promised £5 if he succeeded, and before he took his departure he confided to me privately that he didn't care if he never tasted another mouthful of mutton as long as he lived.

As the months dragged on, and the date approached upon which King must either respond to my challenge or forfeit his title to the belt, public opinion veered round to my side. It was realised that I had been hardly dealt by, and several benefits and testimonials were got up for me. Amongst these latter, the most important was the public presentation to me of a beautifully chased gold cup weighing over one hundred ounces, the gift of Mr. Windham, of Felbrigge Hall, Norwich, upon whose estate my ancestors had been resident for several generations.

The Windham Cup, presented to Mace

This ceremony took place at the Criterion Hall, Leicester Square, and practically everybody in the world of sport who was anybody was there. The orchestra played 'See the Conquering Hero Comes' when I advanced to the centre of the stage to give thanks, which I did while standing before a table whereon were prominently displayed all the other trophies - cups, belts, medals, and so forth - I had won or been presented with in the course of my career.

Shortly after this King allowed his right to the belt to lapse, and immediately I began to be inundated with challenges. Amongst them was one from another mysterious 'Unknown', but this time I was, as you may easily believe, very glad to take him on, the more especially as he put down the very substantial sum of £40 as earnest money.

Of course I covered it, and made sure I was going to have a fight; but again, as on the previous occasion, it all ended in smoke, the 'Unknown' or his backers deciding to forfeit when the time came for staking the remainder of the money. Who the ambitious pugilist was I never knew, but I heard long afterwards that he was an American from Philadelphia.

Personally I would have preferred to have fought Heenan to anybody else, and one day, meeting him accidentally at Owen Swift's public-house in the Haymarket, I asked him point-blank to challenge me. There were a lot of sporting men and pugilists present at the time, including Heenan's old antagonist, Tom Sayers.

The latter upheld me in my request, and offered to find Heenan £500 if he would fight me, but Heenan shook his head. This seemed to anger Sayers, who rose from his seat and made as if to smack Heenan in the face, at the same time exclaiming, but not very loudly: 'If you won't fight Mace, I will'.

The words were not intended for my ears, but I overheard them and called out to him, 'What's that you say, Tom?' Sayers repeated his words, whereupon I said: 'Nothing would give me greater pleasure, Tom, than to fight you. We are both about the same size and weight, and I am sure we should render a good account of ourselves. So to show you that I am in earnest, here is a 'fiver' to bind the match'.

Tom at once covered the note with one of his own for a like amount. But a friend of his who was present joined in the conversation, and said, 'Tom, you promised us that, win or lose with Heenan, you would not fight again'.

There was a lot more argument on both sides, and eventually Tom asked for the return of his fiver. This I at once agreed to, telling him, what was the truth, that it was not his money I wanted, but to fight him, or Heenan, or both of them at suitable intervals.

But it was not to be, although Sayers did presently challenge me, he forfeited almost directly for some reason best known to himself; while Heenan, as I have already stated, preferred meeting King.

Tom Sayers, who retired as Champion of England

Chapter 16
Prize-Fighters and the Law

There soon appeared, however, a candidate in the field who I could see from the first really did mean business.

This was Joe Goss, a provincial man. He came from Wolverhampton, but was fairly well known at the time in fistic circles in London. Amongst other famous fights in which he had proved victorious was one with that prince of hard sloggers, Bodger Crutchley, when no fewer than 120 rounds were fought, the battle lasting 3 hours 20 minutes. He was also the hero of two desperate encounters with Bill Ryall, the Birmingham champion, in one of which he proved victorious, the other being declared a draw by order of the referee after 3 hours and 18 minutes of very quick and punishing work, both combatants being then too weak to do more than feebly push one another about.

Posh Price, my old antagonist, had had to give Goss best, too. But, whereas I beat Mr. Posh in twenty minutes and easily, Goss took more than two hours over the job, and was nearly done for himself into the bargain before he had finished with it. Still, I was not going to take chances. The 'Wolverhampton Wonder', as Goss was nicknamed, might easily prove a very ugly customer to tackle, for his strength was said to be phenomenal, while his hardness, when in proper condition, was such that he could stand almost any amount of punishment without its appearing to have any ill effect on him.

So into training I went, and very hard I worked, for the sum I was to contend for was no less than £1,000, the biggest I had ever a chance of earning through a single fight, and I did not mean to let it slip through my fingers if I could help it.

I very nearly did so, however, and that without ever having a chance to enter the ring at all. It came about in this way. By the articles it was stipulated that neither of us was to scale more than 10st. 10Ib, which was Goss's fighting weight, and which had also been mine. But owing to the easy life I had been leading since my fight with King, I had put on flesh, although neither my trainer nor myself suspected it. Or at least, if such a thought did cross the minds of either of us, we concluded that the training would pull me down all right.

Judge of my dismay, therefore, and of the horror, almost despair, of my trainer, when only three days before the date fixed for the fight, and but forty-eight hours before the official

Joe Goss, the 'Wolverhampton Wonder'

weighing, we discovered, almost by an accident, that I was nearly four pounds too heavy. Here was a quandary. There were no Turkish baths in those days, and to fast would weaken me, and jeopardise my chance of winning.

However, there was no help for it. The decree went forth that neither bite nor sup must pass my lips for two entire days; until, that is to say, I had passed the official weighing test. Besides this, too, I had to submit to be half-baked in a room wherein two enormous fires were kept going night and day, and the blankets that were piled upon me to induce perspiration formed a heap that reached nearly to the ceiling.

Even then I only scraped through by the skin of my teeth. The weighing took place at the 'Greyhound', Waterloo Road, at twelve o'clock in the day, and I got there five minutes before the hour. 'Have a glass of fix, Jem?' was the first salutation, and a friend thrust a foaming goblet under my nose. I would have given £10 to have accepted the kind invitation, but a look from my trainer bade me beware.

And well it was for me that I did so, for although, when I presently seated myself in the weighing-chair, and wore only the thinnest suit of silken fleshings that could be bought for money, I disturbed the balance, and a great shout of 'Forfeit! Forfeit!' went up from the Goss party. However, the disturbance was only temporary, for after I had settled in my seat it was found that I turned the scale at 10st. 9lbs. 14 and three quarter ounces...

The other side at once demanded, as it was such a near thing, that the weights should be tested. This was done, but they were found to be perfectly correct; and I heaved a deep sigh of relief.

One thousand pounds won by one and a quarter ounces. One thousand pounds earned through refusing a glass of champagne.

At least it *would* be won and earned, I reflected, if I succeeded in beating Joe on the morrow. If!

This one little word caused me some uneasiness that night, for I was weak with fasting and much sweating.

I think that of all my battles this was the one which created the greatest excitement beforehand. Goss was regarded as the champion of the Midlands, and consequently many hundreds of people from there flocked into London in his wake.

Even when I went to weigh in at 'The Greyhound', Waterloo Road, excited crowds blocked the entire thoroughfare, completely holding up the traffic. One had to pay a halfpenny toll then to get over Waterloo Bridge, but the rougher element amongst the mob rushed the turnstiles, reducing the poor old tollkeeper to the verge of desperation.

As the day drew to a close and darkness set in matters got worse. The sporting houses all over London were besieged by throngs of people, desirables and undesirables, every one of them actuated, however, by the same determination. They must and would know the name of the station whence the 'special' was to start for the field of battle.

Did a landlord profess ignorance, he stood a very good chance of being maltreated, or of having his bar wrecked. For this reason many who were really not 'in the know' gave the name of a station at haphazard.

But, despite of so many false scents being thus scattered, it became pretty well known by midnight that Paddington was really the rendezvous; and thither, consequently, between that hour and one or two o'clock in the morning, the mob repaired.

And what a mob! I have spoken in a preceding chapter of the one that attended at Fenchurch Street on the occasion of my second fight with King. That was a fairly ruffianly one. But it was as a zephyr to a blizzard by comparison with the one that gathered upon this occasion.

When I arrived with my bodyguard at about 4 a.m. there must have been fully five thousand people, the dregs of London mostly, surrounding the station approaches. Nearly all of them were brandishing bludgeons, or heavy sticks of some description, and the yells and uproar of all kinds made the scene a pandemonium.

We knew that twenty stalwart ring-keepers, ex-pugilists all of them, guarded the station gates, and that once inside we should be all right. But how to get through the mob was the question. To charter a cab would have been worse than useless, for these vehicles were specially spotted by the thieving fraternity, who seized them by the wheels and overturned them, afterwards robbing the unfortunate occupants at their leisure.

Obviously there was but one way, if we did not want to be left behind, and that was to fight our way through. We waited a little while for reinforcements, and then, to the number of about twenty, we dashed into the thick of it. I simply used my fists, and I should think I bowled over a dozen or more of the roughs. Others, however thinking, I suppose, that the occasion warranted it, used knuckle-dusters, life-preservers, and loaded canes.

Old Bill Richardson was our leader, and he was a host in himself. He carried his favourite weapon, a billiard cue sawn in halves, with which he did terrible execution. He told me afterwards, in confidence, that he was afraid he had killed one or two of the thugs. I should not have been surprised, for there were few uglier customers in all London than old Bill when his temper was once roused. He had been a navvy, then a prize-fighter, and, finally, a sporting publican, his house, the 'Blue Anchor', Shoreditch, holding the same relative position in the East End of London as did Nat Langham's in the West.

His strength was such that it passed into a proverb: 'As strong as a bull - or as old Bill Richardson'. He would perform in his own bar-parlour pretty well all the tricks of the modern professional 'strong man', and thought nothing of lifting above his head four 112 lb. weights, two in either hand.

Nevertheless, it took us a full twenty minutes to fight our way through, so it may be judged how savage and determined was the mob. On the platform we found Goss and his crowd who had arrived earlier on the scene and who all bore traces, in their dishevelled clothes, and in some instances bruised faces, of the ordeal they, too, had had to undergo.

We could gaze now from comparative safety over the surging human sea outside, and a terrible sight it was to behold. Even now, after the lapse of nearly half a century, I can see in my mind's eye the vast panorama of upturned faces, brutalised by vice and every vile passion, wanly lit by the big lamps outside the station.

The roaring never wholly ceased, although it died away partially now and then; only, however, to break out again with renewed violence as the mob made one of its periodical attempts to rush the gates, thereby coming in conflict with our guards. There must have been

The riot at Paddington Station

many scores of broken heads amongst London's roughs that day, for the defenders of the gates laid about them unmercifully with the loaded heads of their heavy whalebone whips, so that in one of the last and most determined of the rushes I saw at least a dozen would-be stormers knocked bleeding and senseless to the ground in the space of as many seconds.

At length, to our great relief, we were told by the stationmaster, who evidently began to fear for the safety of himself and staff, to say nothing of the company's property should the mob succeed in breaking through, to take our seats in the waiting special. Hurriedly we did as we were told, the whistle sounded, the wheels began to revolve, and although at that moment a small contingent of the ruffians did manage to break through the barriers, only about a dozen all told succeeded in boarding the train, and these were made to behave themselves on threat of being thrown bodily out of the windows.

I noticed with considerable apprehension that squads of police were in evidence all along the line. At Didcot, the first stop, there must have been fully a score of them. They eyed us curiously, I thought mockingly, but made no attempt to interfere with us.

On again. The sun is well up now, and the day promises to be a perfect one. It is the first of September, the date dedicated to 'St. Partridge', and in the browning woods as we glide by, and out of the bare stubble fields, we can hear the pop-pop-pop of the guns, and see the thin blue wreaths of smoke from the discharges curling lazily upwards in the still autumn air.

Some twenty-five or thirty young 'Varsity' men had joined us at Didcot, having evidently got the tip overnight, and these warned us that the whole official county was roused against us, and that the constabulary had been given strict orders to see that the fight did not come off in Oxfordshire. It was therefore deemed wise to run our special out of this danger zone into Wilts. This was accordingly done, the orders to the driver being to run along until he saw a likely spot and then pull up.

Such a spot was presently found near Wootton Bassett, five miles the other side of Swindon, and here we disembarked, a motley crew of gentleman, bookmakers, undergraduates, sporting publicans, pugilists, and roughs. In a fair daisy-spangled meadow near the line the ring was pitched, but just as all was ready the farmer to whom the land belonged came bustling up, red as a turkey-cock with anger, and demanded to know by whose authority we were there, and how dared we trespass on his property.

Of course, he got jeered at for his pains. Nevertheless, the sturdy old yeoman stood his ground pluckily, placing himself in the middle of the ring and swearing roundly that he would not be moved except by force, and that in that event he would 'have the law on every mother's son of us'. In the end, however, he was 'squared' by a couple of sovereigns and then, all smiles, announced his intention to 'see t' foight'.

Chapter 17
The Fight with Goss Comes Off

But no 'foight' was there to be; at least, not on that spot. For hardly had Goss and I sparred up to one another, ere the police put in an appearance, having ridden over from Swindon. They made no arrests. Indeed, the inspector in charge, who seemed a very decent sort of fellow, volunteered the information that, so far as he personally was concerned, he would be only too pleased to allow the fight to come off, and to himself stop and see it. 'But', he added, 'as you know, gentlemen, orders are orders and must be obeyed'.

Yes. Orders were orders. There was no help for it. To the train! The referee says we will steam a few miles further down the line and try our luck again. But the railway officials will have no more of it. They had fulfilled their part of the contract, they argued, in bringing us to where we then were. That we were not able to bring off the fight after having got there was no fault of theirs. The train was now going back to Paddington. If we liked to come with it, and in it, well and good. If not, why then, well and good too. We could stay where we were.

Logic of this kind was unanswerable, so back to London we journeyed, arriving at Paddington about two o'clock in the afternoon. A number of the crowd that had behaved so outrageously in the early morning were still there, waiting round the station to learn the result of the battle, and their astonishment, when they saw Goss and myself step out from our respective carriages, neither bearing any sign of injury, was naturally very great.

A short consultation was held on the platform, and then the word was passed to those entitled to know that they were to make the best of their way to Fenchurch Street. Instantly every available cab was commandeered, and away eastward we all trailed, four and five in a hansom, from six to ten in and on a growler; hot, vexed, tired, and thoroughly uncomfortable.

Meanwhile, news of what was happening had got wind, and when we arrived at Fenchurch Street we found the station packed with an excited and disorderly crowd of several hundreds of people, all struggling to get tickets to Purfleet, which place, it was generally assumed, was the most likely to see the battle come off.

There was, of course, no question of chartering a 'special' this time, and anybody who chose to book by the 'ordinary', and who could manage to force his way into it, was at perfect liberty to do so. As a result, I should think that fully two thousand people, amongst them being a large contingent of roughs, travelled down, many of them without having previously gone through the formality of paying their fares.

My seconds and I secured a first-class compartment to ourselves by the simple process of pitching out on the platform, one by one, a gang of some half-dozen malodorous and ticketless ruffians who had previously taken possession of it, and so we made the journey in comparative comfort. But in nearly all the other carriages, I heard later on, they were riding eighteen to twenty to the compartment.

Arrived at Purfleet, the order was suddenly given to cross the river to Plumstead Marshes, the idea being to shake off at least a proportion of the rough element. In this, however, we were not very successful. For although some of the swells paid as much as a guinea for the exclusive use of a boat to ferry them across, their 'reserved craft' was almost invariably invaded by a swarm of loafers, who paid nothing. Indeed, it has always been a matter of wonderment to me that no lives were lost, for the tide was running swiftly seaward; the river, especially in the middle, was very choppy and the frail cockleshells in which most of our party had, perforce, to embark were loaded to the gunwales with twice, and often thrice, their proper complement of passengers.

However, save for a ducking here and there, no harm was done; and by five o'clock - just fifteen hours after the majority of us had started the day's outing - the ring was pitched and the battle recommenced.

While we were sparring for an opening I took close stock of Goss, in order to try and ascertain whether the fatigue of the three long railway journeys had told upon him in any way. By rights it ought to have done, for when a man is trained fine for fighting, any unwonted and prolonged hustling about, especially when, as in this case, it is accompanied by lack of proper food, is apt to upset his balance.

Joe, however, I am bound to say, looked as well and fit as any man I ever stood up to, his immensely powerful arms hanging loose, and his huge, slightly bowed, legs planted firm as twin oak saplings on the springy greensward.

As for myself, I cannot, of course, say from my own knowledge how I looked to other people. But as the reader may be interested in the matter, I will quote briefly from a contemporary account of the battle, which I happened to preserve, and to have by me.

'Mace, (so runs the description) *'was the first to pull off his shirt, and then could be seen the grand outlines of his muscular form. There was a buzz of admiration all round the ring. His condition was perfect, and the muscles of his chest, back, and arms looked really spendid in their formidable proportions. Over his shoulder-blades there worked a heap of thews and sinews that looked like nothing so much as a bed of snakes under the skin as he moved with deliberate motion his arms backwards and forwards. From shoulders to waist he was the personification of power, and his appearance fully justified the odds that were freely offered on his chance.'*

I had heard a great deal of talk, prior to entering the ring, about Joe's 'terrible rushes', and expected therefore to meet one of the cyclonic style of fighters, a sort of Pedlar Palmer and John L. Sullivan rolled into one. But, no! Master Joe hung fire most lamentably, and when I pressed him he kept retreating before me until he was on the ropes.

Then, of course, he could go no further. So I closed up, and let him have a spank in the mouth that made him lick his lips and look angry. He tried to counter, but I parried him easily, and let him have it again, this time over the eyebrow, which I cut badly, the blood gushing out all over his face.

I began to think I was having it all my own way, but was undeceived in the fourth round by that most telling of all arguments, a stunning blow in the right eye, which at once began to swell badly. At this there was a tremendous lot of excitement in the Wolverhampton man's corner, tumultuous cheering mingled with cries of 'The Young 'un wins! The Young 'un wins!'

'Does he?' thought I to myself, for I had by this time got my antagonist pretty well sized up. 'Does he?' I don't think so. Just wait a bit'. And with that I retreated, making out as though I were afraid. Master Joe, as I had foreseen, pressed forward exultantly - also rashly - to follow up his advantage, I all the time giving way before him, yet watching for my opportunity.

It came. But not before I was almost on the ropes. Then Goss half-turned his head for a fraction of a second to flash an exultant glance at one of his backers in the inner ring. Instantly I ducked sideways under his guard, sprang erect, and, as he wheeled round to face me, I landed him a swinging left-hander on the side of the jaw that knocked him clean off his pins.

In the sixth round, however, I came within an ace of losing the fight, and, incidentally, my £1,000, through what would have been, had it come off, a quite unintentional foul. I had struck Joe hard and swift in the face with both hands, and was about to follow up with a third stinger, when he suddenly dropped on his knees. The instinct of the fighting animal in me made me depress my arm and bend my body so

Mace lands his left hand

as to be able to deliver the blow at the lower level necessary to damage him in his then position. But luckily, just in the nick of time, I realised what I was about to do, and checked myself with a flourish. Whereat was more cheering, mingled with laughter, in the latter of which I incontinently joined.

I laughed the other side of my face, though, in the eighth round, for Goss 'got the grip of me' and threw me, he falling on the top of me with his full weight, so that all the breath was for the time being pretty well knocked out of my body. This, too, he repeated in the twelfth round. They were terrible falls, and took more out of me than all of his many blows put together.

Still, I had no doubt in my own mind that, barring accidents, I had him beaten. And so, indeed, it proved. For after fighting continuously for the space of one hour and fifty-seven minutes, I got in a blow that proved too much for even his hardness. It was a right-hander on the side of Joe's left jaw, and he spun round and round like a teetotum, then dropped forward on his face insensible, his arms and all the upper part of his body quite still, only his mighty lower limbs twitching once or twice convulsively.

It was fully five minutes before he came to, and his first words were, 'Well done, Jem!' They so affected me that I ran over to his corner and kissed him. Not that he was a pretty object to kiss. Far from it. But I was so elated at my victory that I could have kissed anybody or anything. I also whispered in his ear that he was the best man I ever met in the ring. Which was not the truth, I am sorry to have to confess.

Chapter 18
A Fight Prevented in Ireland

The next challenge I received after defeating Goss was a 'startler'. It came, not from a Briton as I naturally expected, but from a 'Yank', one Joe Coburn, who called himself Champion of America. Of course I accepted, and great was the curiosity amongst English pugilists, myself included, to see the challenger.

He arrived in London in due course, accompanied by his backers and friends, and proved himself at least as cute as the majority of his countrymen. The sum for which we were to do battle was £1,000, and Coburn's backers and advisers raised all sorts of objections as to the stakeholders. Then, when these were settled, they insisted that the fight should take place, not in England, but in Ireland, under the ridiculous plea that their man, being an Irish-American, would not get fair play in this country.

In vain it was pointed out that all previous fights for the championship had invariably been held on English soil, and further, that the

Joe Coburn

danger from interference by the police, although it was admittedly great in this country, would be far greater in Ireland. They listened patiently to all we had to urge. But they remained obdurate. The battle, they insisted, should come off in Ireland, or nowhere.

My backers thereupon wanted me to retire from the business altogether. But this I had little mind to do. I had seen Coburn, and had no fears about not being able to beat him.

'Why', I argued, 'should I be asked to throw away the chance of winning £1,000?' So in the end to Ireland we went, and put up at a Dublin hotel so as to be handy to the proposed field of battle, which was close to a place called Gould's Cross, on the road to Thurles.

Almost from the very first moment of landing, however, I became convinced in my own mind that there was not going to be any fight. The people were friendly enough, and obviously anxious for all to go smoothly. But the police were dead against us. We were shadowed wherever we went. And not only were the civil authorities thus hostile to us, but so also were the ecclesiastical ones. The priests everywhere warned their flocks against in any way countenancing, much less going to see, 'so brutal and disgusting an exhibition'. Finally the railway company, when asked to provide a special train to carry us to the proposed rendezvous, curtly refused.

The upshot of it was that the whole affair fizzled out. The Americans, however, remained in Dublin after we had left, and chose to go through the solemn farce of travelling to Gould's Cross - where they were received on the station platform by a hundred or more constabulary all armed with carbines - and there pitching a ring. Into this Coburn then threw his glove, as a challenge, and there being, of course, no response, he thereupon claimed the victory and the stakes.

These last, needless to say, he did not get; for the match, having fallen through without either of the principals being to blame, each man had his money returned him. With true Yankee 'cuteness' however, Coburn had stipulated to receive £100 for his expenses, and this he got, half of it being my money, or rather the money put up by my backers.

It was some time after this fiasco that Goss challenged me again. He had never been satisfied with his beating, but kept going about saying that he could have licked me had he been allowed to fight me his own way instead of having to follow the bad advice of his backers and seconds. Something like this he repeated in my hearing, whereupon I went up to him and said, 'Look here, Joe, what is the good of keeping on saying that. It only causes people to laugh at you. You know I can't challenge *you*. But if you think you can lick me, why in the name of goodness don't *you* challenge *me*?' 'So I will', he replied with some heat; and with that we parted - to meet again next day and sign articles.

The second battle of mine with Goss, if battle indeed it could be called, was I suppose one of the most extraordinary ever recorded in the history of the Prize Ring. It came about in this way. While I was yet in training, and only a few days prior to the fight, I had the misfortune to severely strain my instep. No amount of rubbing with embrocations and liniments seemed to do it any good, and the reader may imagine, if he can, the state of mind I was in, knowing, as I did, or thought I did, that if any information concerning the accident were to reach Goss's ears the battle was as good as lost.

By the doctor's orders I wore an elastic stocking, but it offered me little relief, and on the day of the fight I was quite lame. This lameness I had, of course, to disguise, and I don't think I ever suffered greater agony in my life than in doing so. Obviously, under such circumstances, my proper, indeed, only course, was to play a waiting game, and trust to something happening. This I did. But when I first took my stand in front of my formidable opponent I said to myself that the fight, so far as I was concerned, was over before it was begun.

To my unbounded surprise and astonishment, however, Joe seemed even more determined than I was to act on the defensive.

We sparred and we sparred, and I have no doubt that, considered as sparring, it was a very pretty exhibition indeed. Only - it was not what the spectators came to see. They began to grow impatient.

Luckily there was on this particular occasion a marked absence of the rough element. And well it was for us that it was so, otherwise the ring would almost certainly have been rushed and ourselves mobbed. As it was, the shouts and yells of disapprobation and menace were deafening.

Ten minutes passed by, twenty, thirty, forty, and never a blow had been struck. Was ever such a thing heard of in a championship battle before? No wonder the crowd abused us roundly. From their point of view we most certainly deserved it. And all the while I was wondering why on earth Joe didn't sail in and make mincemeat of me. Every moment I expected that he would.

He didn't, however; and in the end the referee declared the match a draw. On the way back I got Goss by himself, determined to satisfy my curiosity at all hazards.

'Joe, old man', I said, 'why didn't you force the fighting?'

He did not answer the question, but countered it instead with another.

'Why didn't you?' he asked.

'Well', said I, 'to tell you the truth, I'm dead lame'.

And I pulled down my sock and showed him my swollen and discoloured ankle. I was prepared for him to start and look surprised; but I did not think to see him so utterly dumbfounded and flabbergasted as he was.

'Crikey!', he exclaimed, using a favourite expression of his. 'Oh, crikey, Jem! Well I'm blowed! Oh, crikey!'

He seemed incapable of doing more than utter these and similar ejaculations, so I pulled him up short by asking him again why he hadn't forced the fighting when he saw me hang back.

'Why?', he said. 'Why? You want to know why I didn't force the fighting. Well, for the same reason that you didn't; because I couldn't. I sprained my wrist lifting the dumb-bells the day before yesterday. Look!' And with that he rubbed from off his right lower forearm some pink paint, and I could see the flesh and muscles beneath showing blue and bruised.

So that was it. Needless to say, we laughed long and heartily. And, indeed, the situation would have not disgraced a scene from a comic opera. Here were two trained gladiators, standing up to do battle with one another in a contest upon which thousands of pounds had been staked, and both of us as incapable of fighting as a couple of pap-fed kids.

The public, however, didn't appear to think it funny; nor the Press, which I suppose represents the public. Some of the sporting papers were especially hard on us, although why they should have been so I cannot for the life of me see to this day, for the match having been declared a draw nobody lost any bets. Even our backers asked for their money back and got it. The only people who had reason to complain, it seemed to me, were those who had purchased tickets for the special that conveyed them to the scene of the proposed fight, and even they got, in exchange for their couple of guineas, a very pretty little exhibition of sparring. As for me, I was all my training expenses to the bad, as was also, of course, Goss, and we were both badly hurt into the bargain. Nevertheless, as I said, we were roughly handled in the papers, even *Punch* joining in with the following rather witty little impromptu, written, I was given to understand at the time, by the celebrated Sir Frank Burnand:

'Jem Mace and Joe Goss in their last little brush

Displayed a most delicate grace,

For Mace merely Goss-sipp'd o'er claret and punch,

And Goss only made a Grim Mace'

Naturally the affair could not rest here. For the sake of both our reputations it was now more than ever necessary that there should be a fight to the finish. So Joe issued another formal challenge, the battle to come off within three months of the date of the draw.

Of course I was bound in a sense to accept. And I was anxious to, too. At the same time, however, I was considerably worried about my injured foot.

As may well be imagined, the ordeal I had gone through had not improved matters. Indeed, from an ordinary but very painful strain, it had now developed into something very like a sprain; and, as everybody knows, three months is none too long a time in which to effect a thorough cure of a sprained ankle.

In the end, however, I agreed to fight within the time limit mentioned above, provided that Goss, on his part, would agree to meet me in a sixteen foot ring instead of the large twenty-four foot ring then generally in vogue.

This, of course, was so that I should not be obliged to run about after him so much as I had done on the first occasion. He did not like it at first, but eventually he agreed.

'Anything you like', he said brusquely, 'so that the fight comes off.'

'Oh, it'll come off all right, never you fear', I snapped in reply, for I was nettled at his tone and manner. And it did come off, too, as I shall show in the next chapter; and settled, once for all, the question as to which was the better man.

Nevertheless, it looked at one time as if there was going to be yet another fizzle and for this reason - almost on the very eve of the fight I managed to get myself clapped in gaol.

Chapter 19
My Third and Last Fight with Joe Goss

It was very provoking that as the date for my third and final encounter with Goss was fast approaching I should find myself in gaol.

And the funny part of it was that I, who had acted as principal in so many fights, served my first, last, and only term of imprisonment, not for fighting but for aiding and abetting a fight.

I had been persuaded, against my better judgment, into acting as one of the seconds in a match for £50 aside that came off in the neighbourhood of Walsall. It was not a contest of any particular notoriety or importance. But the police got wind of it, and arrested the lot of us.

Fourteen days in the local gaol was my sentence, and very hard lines, indeed, I thought it, especially when, on the second day of my incarceration, a travelling fair came to the town and pitched in a field adjoining the prison.

Just try and put yourself - in imagination, of course - in my place. Through my cell window came the sound of riot and revelry, the music, the laughter, the hoarse shouting of the showmen, the screaming of the sirens, the grinding and the rattling of the roundabouts. 'Not agreeable sounds', I hear you exclaim. No, perhaps not - to you. But to me they were as the very breath of my nostrils.

For, you see, I had been brought up amongst shows of the kind, and had travelled with them practically all my life. It was my *home* that had been brought to the gaol wherein I was, and dumped down within earshot.

Within earshot, but out of the range of vision, for the one small window was high up near the ceiling, and heavily glazed. Could anything be more tantalising?

Not a wink of sleep did I get the first night it pitched there. Nor the second. On the third I could stand it no longer. I begged a warder to fetch the governor to me, saying I had an important communication to make to him.

That gentleman came to my cell in due course. He was a retired military officer with a wooden leg, very strict and stern-looking, but not, I think a bad sort. Also, like most of his class and calling in those days, he was a lover, if not actually a patron, of the noble art of self-defence as exemplified in the prize ring.

For these reasons, probably, he asked me, not unkindly, and addressing me by name, what it was I wanted. 'If you please, sir', I replied, 'you've got a fair here, and if you wouldn't mind letting me go out for about two hours I'll give you my word of honour to come back'.

Now, I made this request in all good faith, and was quite unprepared for its effect upon the worthy governor. He turned all shades of red, from pale pink to dark purple, until I thought he was going to have an apoplectic stroke. Then he started spitting out a string of sentences that were only half intelligible, but the purport of which I was able to gather from such stray words as did reach me, amongst which 'unbounded cheek' and 'infernal impudence', repeated over and over again, figured prominently. Finally, he stopped short for sheer lack of breath, and then, the humour of the thing seeming to suddenly strike him, he burst into hearty laughter.

'Good story, sir! Good story!' I heard him muttering as he stumped his way back along the corridor. 'Gad, sir, I must tell 'em at the club to-night'. Next day I was transferred to an upper cell, where was a window, barred but unglazed, and from which a view could be had over the fair grounds. Nevertheless, I was not sorry when, a little later, the showmen packed up and took their departure.

As soon as I was released I resumed my interrupted training, journeying to a quiet spot near Liverpool for the purpose. I quickly discovered that my short incarceration had done me no harm. Indeed, to tell the truth, I believe I felt all the better for it. Certainly my lameness had disappeared. So I set to work with a will, walking, running, rowing, varied by occasional bouts with the gloves and punching the sack - there was no ball-punching in those days.

As a result, I never felt in better fettle in my life than on the eve of the battle; and I was confident of winning, if only it were allowed to come off. There was, however, some doubt about this, for it was rumoured in London that warrants had been issued for the arrest of both Goss and myself.

Consequently, we lay very low, Joe hiding in the East End in coster's rig-out; while I thought it better to get myself up as a typical swell of the period - well-cut light cloth trousers topping a pair of exceedingly thin patent-leather boots, a fully buttoned-up frock coat, large flowing cravat of the type then fashionable, single eye-glass, and a sparkling 'topper' of the chimney-pot brand.

Thus arrayed, I travelled to London from Liverpool overnight, in company with a friend of mine, who was similarly attired, and together we put up at a small, but very select, private hotel near St. Paul's Cathedral. The fight was to come off down the Thames, and a steamer had been chartered, the railway company having declined to furnish us with a special train on any terms.

The starting-place for the boat was Hungerford Bridge, but I judged it wiser not to venture there. Instead, I made my way with my companion to St. Paul's Pier, passing on the road several policemen, none of whom, however, appeared to recognise me. A quarter to five was the time arranged for starting, and reckoned on the steamer being abreast of where we were by about 5a.m.

So she was, but I had rather overdone my disguise, and none of those on board recognised me. As a result the captain, seeing, as he thought, only a couple of waiting strangers who might, for aught he knew to the contrary, be police officers in mufti, made no attempt to stop his boat, but kept straight on down the river.

I was too flabbergasted by this totally unexpected eventuality to do more than wildly wave my umbrella. But my companion, who luckily possessed a voice like a foghorn, roared across the muddy water a volley of ejaculations, the purport of which may easily be guessed.

As a result of this, aided possibly by my excited gesticulations, those on board seemed to realise that at the very least we must have some important communication to make. Slowly, and to our great relief, the little steamer, packed as we could now see from stem to stern with a dense crowd of spectators, slowed down, and then stopped. `Put her astern', yelled the skipper, evidently in no very good humour.

'Now then, gentlemen, jump', he added, as the boat grazed the pier.

Jump it was, and, luckily, we landed safe aboard. Even then, however, nobody seemed to recognise me, and it was not until I put my great pickled hands up to my face, with the idea of hiding the grin that *would* come on, that a great yell went up from those nearest me, 'Damme, if it isn't old Jem!'

The recognition over, as likewise multitudinous hand-shakes, I strolled to the upper deck and surveyed the assemblage. Seldom had I seen a more orderly or respectable lot. We looked, indeed, more like an Exeter Hall excursion party than what we really were. But this, I afterwards learned, was largely due to Nat Langham's elaborate arrangements for excluding the rough element. Also, perhaps, the high price of the tickets - three guineas apiece - may have had something to do with it.

Anyhow, there it was. From start to finish there was no rowdyism of any kind whatever, a welcome change from the terrible scenes at Paddington which disgraced my first encounter with the redoubtable Joe. Even the disembarkation, which is usually, on these river-trips, marked by some little pushing and hustling, as each member of the party tries to be first on the scene of action and thus secure a good place, was quite orderly and decorous.

As had been previously agreed upon, the ring measured sixteen feet only, instead of the usual twenty-four, and when we faced one another I knew, at all events, that anyhow Master Joe had not much room for his favourite dodging tactics. There were, too, no seconds inside the ring to get in the way, these taking their places outside, as was usual in contests fought in these smaller rings.

Eight o'clock, I remember, was chiming from some nearby clock when we toed the scratch. 'Now, Joe, look out for yourself, I cried, as we squared up, after the customary preliminary handshake. 'Look out for thyself, said Joe. And at it we went, neither of us waiting to do any 'weaving', *i.e.* fancy in-and-out sparring of the preliminary kind.

I drew 'first blood' with a spanking blow on the mouth, and a mighty roar of cheering went up from my supporters round the ring, for there had been heavy wagering on this particular side issue. Next I cut his right eyebrow to the bone, the blood spurting from a gash extending half-way across his forehead. The sight of this decided my tactics. I visited it again and again, whenever I got the opportunity, bruising the exposed bone, and enlarging the wound each time, till I had him nearly mad with the pain and fury of it.

He fought as gamely as ever though, and more fiercely, I thought. None ever battled more grimly for his backers' money than did Joe on this occasion. But it was no good. In the little ring we were fighting in, I had him at my mercy, so that in twenty minutes he was manifestly a beaten man, and there were loud shouts of 'Take him away'.

And, indeed, there was no doubt that the sponge ought to have been skied at this point. But Jack Baldock, Goss's second, would not hear of it, although I personally appealed to him to do so, and pointed to Joe, who was staggering all over the place like a drunken man, his hands up and in proper position, it is true, but he making no attempt to use them, either for offence or defence.

Under these circumstances I had not the heart to hit him again, but contented myself with walking away whenever he staggered in my direction; and presently, as I had foreseen, he stumbled, and fell of his own accord and, being unable to rise, was counted out by the referee.

They carried him to his corner, and at that moment the plucky fellow recovered from the swoon into which he had fallen, and, pushing his seconds to one side, wanted to renew. He was a pitiable spectacle, his face one big bruise, his forehead an open wound through which the bone showed, his mouth distorted, his nose swollen to thrice its proper size.

His seconds reasoned with him, and I went over to his corner and shook hands. This he seemed to me to do very unwillingly, and I do not think that he ever quite forgave me for beating him. He realised that he had met his master, however, as the following incident, which occurred a few months later, will show.

I had been in London with a friend, and as I was resting at the time we had been doing the rounds. At one of the many sporting houses which then existed in the vicinity of the Haymarket, a couple of burly sea captains, not knowing who we were, chose to fasten a quarrel with us.

Now, I always made it a rule to avoid a personal encounter with a stranger whenever possible, a rule which was, I think, observed by most of the better class of pugilists at that time. You see, we knew our own skill and quickness, and, according to the etiquette of our profession, it was made to savour of cowardice to use them on a tyro in the art of self-defence, or even on anybody who was only moderately skilful.

Nevertheless, there is a limit to all forbearance, and on this occasion the limit was reached, and passed. They got a warning. They got several warnings, in fact. And then, as they refused to listen to reason, they got what they asked for, namely, a good hiding.

Even then, however, I did not enlighten them as to my identity, and they, burning for revenge, went and enlisted the services of Joe Goss on their behalf, the three starting out on a tour of the West End in search of us. They found us at the Cambrian Stores, near Leicester Square. 'Here they are! Here they are!' exclaimed the seamen. 'Where?' said Goss. 'Why, there', pointing through a half-open door to the table in the inner room where we were sitting. 'Why, that's Jem Mace!' exclaimed Joe. 'Hit 'im a thick 'un? Not me! Not for fifty quid! I've had enough of him'. And with that he made off, and so did the seamen.

To return, however, to the day of the fight. This was all over by half-past eight, having lasted barely the half-hour, and as I had suffered scarcely any facial disfigurement, and felt, moreover, perfectly fresh and well, I determined to return that same day to Liverpool, where I was proprietor of some pleasure gardens, known popularly as the Strawberry Grounds.

This decision was arrived at purely on business grounds, and I was quite unprepared for the reception that awaited me. I suppose there must have been fully ten thousand people round and in the station, and I could hear the roar of their cheering, like the sound of waves beating upon a sea beach, long before the train by which I was travelling drew up at the arrival platform.

On getting out, I was seized and carried shoulder high to a carriage-and-four, in which, preceded by a brass band, and followed by cheering multitudes, I was driven round the city. At night I was entertained to a banquet, at which over one hundred guests, including, I may say, some of the principal citizens of Liverpool, sat down.

Altogether it was a glorious day, topped off with an equally glorious evening, the only drawback, so far as I was concerned, being that the company would insist upon my making a speech. This is an ordeal I have always shrank from. However, on this occasion, I did manage to stammer out a few disjointed remarks, a feat which so delighted one enthusiastic admirer of mine who was present, that he insisted on ordering and paying for six dozen bottles of champagne. These were all uncorked, and the contents poured into a huge silver bowl, a sort of heirloom of the house where we were dining, the wine being afterwards ladled out in tumblers, like punch, and drunk by the assembled guests upstanding in my honour. I am not sure whether all the pouring back and forth it underwent improved the 'fizziness' of the champagne, or whether the reverse was the case. I rather fancy it was the latter. But, anyhow, they drank it all down to the very last drop, and then sang, 'For he's a jolly good fellow'. Heigh ho! Those were merry times.

Chapter 20
Tom Sayers and other Memories

They were also money-making times, the public simply swarming up to my place from all over Liverpool and its environs, so that the takings exceeded for some time £300 a day, a full third of which was clear profit. I used to put on a show of the sort now known as an assault-at-arms, and paid good round sums to the more famous of the old-time pugilists to give exhibitions of boxing.

Amongst those who came to the place, I remember, when I first took it over, was Tom Sayers, but he only stayed a very little while, for he had by this time, I am sorry to say, given way to drink, and was, in consequence, but the wreck of his former self. In his cups, too, he was apt to be very quarrelsome and offensive, as witness the following little incident.

Tom had been 'boozing' all day in the parlour of a certain little 'pub' frequented by sporting men, and I had been sent to try and get him home. As a drunken man frequently will, he resented my well-meant interference, and started abusing me roundly.

In the middle of one of his worst tirades, his eye happened to light on a picture which hung over the mantelpiece, wherein his portrait figured side by side with mine and Heenan's.

Taking up his stick, Tom staggered to the picture, and touching the likeness of the 'Benicia Boy' (as Heenan used to be called) said, 'He's a good man'. Then, touching his own portrait, 'And he's a good man, but this', he continued, indicating myself, 'is a bloomin' duffer'. And with that he drove the point of his stick through the face of the portrait.

My first, and not unnatural instinct, was to knock him down. But I restrained myself, and very glad I was afterwards, for he died a few months later, poisoned by drink, at the early age of thirty-eight.

At about the time of his death there was a great campaign being carried on by a section of the Press against prize fighting and prize-fighters, and Tom was pointed at as a typical 'awful example', the inference being that professional pugilists were all, or nearly all, short-lived on account of their excesses. As a matter of fact, the reverse rather holds good, for of all the long roll of England's champions from the time of Broughton to my own, only six have failed to reach the age of fifty.

Tom Sayers attacks Mace's portrait

They were Tom Johnson, who died at forty-seven, Ben Gaunt at forty-six, Harry Broome at thirty-nine, Tom Sayers at thirty-eight, H. Pearce ('The Game Chicken') at thirty-two, and Jem Belcher. In all these cases, however, death was hastened either by accident or by reckless dissipation.

On the other hand, John Broughton reached his eighty-sixth year, Jem Ward his eighty-fourth, John Gully his eighty-first, John Jackson his seventy-seventh, Dan Mendoza his seventy-fourth, Bendigo his seventieth, and Tom Cribb his sixty-eighth year on April 8th last. I may be wrong, but I do not think these figures could be beaten in any other profession or occupation.

To return to Sayers, however, I should like to say that he was, when in his prime, one of the gamest and fastest fighters I ever saw put up a hand. He was, though, most deceptive in appearance, his arms being no thicker than a girl's. Yet his hitting powers were terrific, and his small, hard, sharp knuckles gashed like the edge of a razor.

I have often wondered what would have been the result of a fight between him and myself, and after his battle with Heenan, as the reader is already aware, I tried my best to induce him to meet me. But Tom would have none of it, and I do not blame him, for he was then in receipt of an allowance, the interest on a sum of about three thousand pounds which had been subscribed by his friends and admirers, and this was only paid him on condition that he refrained from entering the ring again.

I suppose that the two years succeeding the third and last of my fights with Goss were the most prosperous of my life from a financial standpoint. I had only to show myself to earn money. And as fast as I earned it I put it into all sorts of enterprises, so that in a very little while I had over a dozen irons in the fire, being at one and the same time a circus proprietor, publican, bookmaker, racehorse-owner, showman, and I don't know what else besides.

The management of these various businesses naturally necessitated me being much away from home and it was owing to this that I missed being present at the death-bed of the beautiful and talented Adah Isaacs Menken, about whom, and whose career, I had something to say in a previous chapter. We had always been great 'pals', although it was my cousin, Pooley Mace, she chiefly favoured.

However, when she felt her end approaching, she expressed a wish to see both of us, and letters were written and telegrams sent from her flat in Paris to all sorts of places where it was thought we were likely to be. But, as luck would have it, none of them reached either of us in time. The same fate overtook, too, I afterwards heard, other messages which were sent off to certain old-time friends; with the result that the equestrian queen, who had once taken all London by storm, and who had reigned so long as the public idol and the fashionable beauty of the day, died in a foreign land, forsaken and alone.

I was sick and sad, and sorry when the news at last reached me - for, of course, I would have gone to her had I known - and this led indirectly to my fighting one of the few battles I ever allowed myself to indulge in outside the prize-ring. A newspaper containing a brief notice of her death had been handed to me by a friend who knew of our relations, as I was returning from a race-meeting; I think it was Doncaster.

At the station I got into an empty compartment, feeling pretty blue, and at once began to conjure up visions of the dead actress as she was when I last saw her, in all the peerless beauty of her radiant womanhood, at Astley's Amphitheatre. As luck would have it, however, just as I was in the middle of one of the most delicious and beautiful of my reminiscent day-dreams, there burst into the compartment where I was, two burly miners. They had apparently met with bad luck backing the 'gee-gees', and at once began bewailing their misfortunes in some of the foulest language I ever heard fall from the lips of a human being.

Now, ordinarily, I don't suppose I should have taken much notice, beyond at all events, changing carriages at the next stopping-place. A prize-fighter gets inured to that sort of thing.

But just then their blackguardism irritated me beyond endurance. It seemed a sort of sacrilege against the dead. And I ordered them, somewhat curtly and roughly I am afraid, to hold their tongues.

One of them did as he was bid, especially when I explained half-apologetically a minute or so later that I had lost a dear friend, and was greatly upset. But the other fellow started to abuse me, and when I left the compartment, having arrived at my destination, he also got out, and followed me up, spoiling for a fight. So in the end I let him have one.

Gad, though, but he was game! With the first hit I smashed his nose, and afterwards I nearly punched the life out of him before he would acknowledge himself beaten. Of course, however, he had to give in in the end. Then he shook me by the hand, and exclaimed, 'By gum, mon, but tha'rt a foighter, and no misteek; why, th'owt to foight Jem Mace'.

'I *am* Jem Mace', I answered quietly. Whereat his astonishment, likewise his admiration, knew no bounds, and he begged of me to walk with him to the village where he lived - it was only about a mile or so distant - in order that he might show me to his mates and convince them that he owed his defeat, not to any ordinary common or garden bruiser, but to the Champion of England himself.

The reader may possibly wonder how I found time to look after all the multifarious ventures I had on hand at this period of my career, and at the same time attend to the main business of my life, which was prize-fighting. My answer is that there was then no prize-fighting to be done. Indeed, my third battle with Goss is generally regarded as being the last prize fight on British soil.

The reasons for this death-knell of what was once the favourite sport of all classes of Englishmen are not far to seek. For some time previously, I regret to say, the prize ring, and everything connected with it, had been going downhill. There was no longer the same high standard of honour in connection with it that there was when I was a young man. Fights 'on the cross' were frequent, and this, together with the disgraceful rowdyism which seemed to be well-nigh inseparable from most of the later battles for the championship, served to alienate the good old race of sport-loving noblemen and gentlemen who were once its chief supporters.

Their places were taken largely by sporting publicans, some of whom were very good fellows indeed, but some of whom, on the other hand, were not. Trickery amongst these latter was rampant. They would get up a match, sell perhaps two or three hundred tickets for a 'special' excursion to see it at from two to four guineas apiece, and in the end, after all, there would be no fight, the unwary speculators being, of course, diddled out of their money.

Other even worse practices there were, of which I could write if I liked, but what is the good? Prize fighting in England has been dead, so far as this country is concerned, for these forty years and more, and there is an end of it. Other times, other manners. Under present conditions it would be manifestly impossible to revive it. And even if it were not impossible, I am of the opinion that it would be eminently undesirable.

When I say, however, that my battle was the last prize-fight on British soil, I must not be understood as saying that there were none attempted to be brought off. On the contrary, I myself received several challenges subsequently, and made several matches. One of these was with Joe Wormald, a good enough man in a second-rate way, but nowhere near my form.

For this reason I was not at all surprised when at the last moment he claimed to have sprained his wrist, and allowed me to pick up the forfeit money, £120, a nice little bit of 'ready' and easily earned, for I had not even gone into training, believing from the first that he did not mean to toe the scratch.

A challenge issued shortly afterwards by O'Baldwin was, however, a far more serious matter. He was nicknamed 'The Irish Giant', and was, indeed, a tremendous fellow, standing six feet five and three-quarter inches high, and weighing, when in fighting condition, something like two hundred pounds. He was known to be game, too, having fought several desperate battles with men of proved ability, and I anticipated a pretty tough job. From the very beginning, however, we had the greatest difficulty in evading the attentions of the police. They dogged us everywhere; and although we tried every trick we knew to shake them off, they seemed to follow us up by instinct from one part of the country to another.

I remember, for instance, that one day when I was training on top of Hindhead, then about as wild and desolute a spot as it would be possible to conceive of, I thought I saw something moving amongst the heather that covers all the bottom of a big cauldron-like depression known as 'The Devil's Punchbowl'. Suspicious and fearful, I climbed down to investigate. And there, sure enough, was a lurking 'bobby'.

However, on the eve of the battle, what with dodging and turning here, there, and everywhere, I thought I had succeeded in getting the better of them. I came into London disguised, and, without letting a soul know, drove straight to a small private hotel, where I had a meat-tea.

Here, as had been previously arranged, I was joined by my principal second, Bos Tyler, and by my cousins, Gus and Pooley Mace. After they had refreshed the inner man, we all four drove to Herne Hill, so as to be ready to take the train next morning to the place of combat, which it had been decided was to be somewhere down the London, Chatham and Dover line.

We took up our quarters in the house of the stationmaster, a man who we knew we could trust, and by eight o'clock - for it was my custom to keep early hours on the night preceding a fight - I was in bed and sound asleep. Tyler and my two cousins came up to the same room, as they informed me later, about nine, and all three lay down on the floor without removing their clothes.

By eleven o'clock all was still, the rest of the household having retired to rest, when there came a sudden knock at the front door, followed by heavy footsteps, and in a trice the police were amongst us. There must have been a dozen of them, an inspector marching at their head.

'What do you want?' asked Pooley, of this latter.

'I want Jem Mace, and there he is over there', was the reply, and at the same time he pointed to where I was sitting up in bed in my nightshirt, blinking and rubbing my eyes. Now, the police were twelve to four at least, and, moreover, they had the law on their side. The obviously sensible thing to have done, therefore, would have been to have surrendered myself.

But one doesn't always do the sensible things one ought to do in this life, especially when one is suddenly awakened out of a sound sleep, as I had been.

Moreover, I was sore and savage at having been trapped. So the long and short of it was that instead of going quietly, or, indeed, going at all just then, I leapt to my feet and on to the floor, dashed out the lamp with one hand, while with the other I hurled a heavy oaken chair that stood by my bedside full in the centre of the group of grinning bobbies.

They made, as in duty bound, one blind rush for me in the darkness, but only succeeded in catching hold of my shirt, which I left in their hands.

The next instant, naked as the day I was born, I had taken a flying leap through an open window that looked out on to the street. I did not get far though, which was perhaps lucky for me, considering the state I was in. Other policemen had surrounded the house although I did not know it, and me being dazed with the half darkness, and shaken by my flying jump from the window, was easily taken. In fact, I ran right into the arms of a burly chap who had been lying in wait behind some shrubbery, and who had me down and the handcuffs on me, almost before I knew I was being collared.

By this time it was nearly midnight, and we were driven rapidly through the quiet streets in two cabs to Marlborough Street police-station. There the inspector who took the charge refused to entertain the idea of bail, so that we were locked up in the cells all night, to appear the next morning before the magistrate.

That worthy took, or pretended to take, a very serious view of the matter. He read us a long lecture on the evils of prize-fighting, and after threatening to send me to prison for twelve months, wound up by binding me over in the sum of £1,000, myself in £500, and two sureties of £250 each. These, however, on my giving an undertaking not to fight again in England during the next two years, he reduced to £300 and £150 each respectively.

Chapter 21
I Go to America

An end, for some time to come at all events, was thus put to my career as a prize-fighter so far as this country was concerned. What wonder, therefore, that I turned my eyes longingly to the United States of America, where the noble art, moribund in Great Britain, was beginning to be greatly practised and thought of?

Accordingly, I devoted the next eighteen months to settling up my affairs in Liverpool and elsewhere, and, after a brief rest and a much-needed holiday, sailed for New York arriving there towards the end of 1869. I had scarcely set my foot on shore when I received a challenge from a man named Tom Allen, who claimed to be the Champion of America, to fight him for £2,000 and the Championship of the World.

As a fight was precisely what I wanted and had come there for, I was naturally delighted. I replied the same day accepting the challenge, and after the usual negotiations, articles were duly signed, the fight being fixed to come off at New Orleans in May following.

This Tom Allen, I should explain, was not an American, but an Englishman. He had emigrated to New York some years previously, and had fought several hard battles, both on British and American soil, in all of which he had proved himself victorious. He was therefore likely, I considered, to prove himself no mean antagonist. So, some two months prior to the date of the battle, I withdrew myself from the delights of the Bowery and Broadway, and went into training at a place called Magnolia, in the State of Alabama.

My cousin Pooley, who looked after me, had hired a hut of an old negro in the heart of a pine forest, and here, day after day, we raced, boxed, jumped, wrestled, and punched the bag, without a soul being the wiser. I could not help, however, sighing for my old training-quarters on Newmarket Heath, for the heat where I was was well-nigh intolerable, and at night I was eaten up by mosquitoes.

For these reasons I was not sorry when the day of battle arrived. Yet I was somewhat anxious, too, for ugly stories were afloat of the hatred borne to all Englishmen by certain sections of the American populace. Several times latterly had men of my nationality been attacked and maltreated when engaged in perfectly fair fights with native-born Americans, and in some cases revolvers and bowie-knives

Tom Allen

had been used. Of course, as I have already explained, upon this occasion it was a case of Englishman v. Englishman nominally, but Tom, having declared his intention of becoming an American citizen, and taken out his papers, was looked upon as already more than half a Yank, and popular feeling was all in his favour.

My backers and seconds, however, knew what they were about. It was they who had insisted upon New Orleans as the place of battle, that city being situated more than a thousand miles from New York and nearly as far from Pittsburgh, where Tom had his home. As a result of these tactics the roughs were kept away through being unable to afford the long, and consequently expensive railway journey, so that it was quite a high-class crowd that gathered round the ring on the morning of the eventful day.

To me the sight was as pretty as it was strange. Above our heads, in place of English oak and elm, were orange trees and palms. The grass under our feet was not green but yellow. While all round, instead of waving cornfields or smooth pasture lands, were vast level sugar-cane plantations, varied by cotton-fields, and garden-like expanses wherein the tobacco plant flourished luxuriantly.

Nor were the spectators less objects of interest to me than the surroundings. Never in all my experience had I seen or imagined so picturesque and motley an assemblage. Men of all nationalities, seemingly, were there, and of all colours certainly. Creole dandies, glossy-coated and patent-leather booted, jostled bronzed backwoodsmen in homespun. Broad-hatted planters, in suits of white nankeen, were cheek by jowl with smartly-togged 'sports' from New York and St. Louis. The Chicago baseball club were there to a man, in their white and crimson playing colours. While the Louisiana Jockey Club, which had its headquarters in New Orleans, had turned out in its full strength, each member clad in correct morning costume - frock coat, light trousers, and top-hat.

And mingling with these aristocrats of the ringside were numbers of plantation negroes, some jet black, some brown to pale yellow, but all attired in the most variegated and brilliant cotton clothing, similar to that which is worn, or rather which used to be worn, by the nigger minstrels on Margate Sands.

But all the glittering panorama faded from my vision the instant that I stepped into the ring and stood face to face with my opponent. 'For', I kept saying to myself, 'supposing I lose this, my first fight in America, then is my career finished here, as in England, and might as well make up my mind to retire from the ring'.

And, mind you, Tom was a good man. He had fought and beaten some of the best boxers America could produce. Besides, he was only twenty-six, whereas I was thirty-nine, and thirteen years counts for much when it comes to prize-fighting. For these reasons I was not altogether without misgivings.

The first couple of rounds, however, put confidence into me. I could see he was no match for me, and I think he must have known it. Only, as he claimed to be Champion of America, he had to fight me or forfeit the title.

I have described so many of my battles that think it hardly worthwhile to give the full details of any more of them, for one prize fight is, after all, very much like another prize fight. Suffice it to say that my battle with Tom Allen very much resembled the one I had with Sam Hurst, 'the Stalybridge Infant', in that I had it almost all my own way from the beginning, and inflicted the most frightful and disfiguring punishment on my opponent, while receiving practically no injury whatever myself.

His poor face I smashed and mangled out of recognition. Both his eyes were closed to slits, so that he could barely see. And in the last round, with two terrific hits, I dislocated first his jaw and then his shoulder, after which, of course, there was nothing for his seconds but to sky the sponge. This they accordingly did, after forty-four minutes' exceedingly fast fighting. They carried poor Tom from the field nearly senseless, with a horse rug wrapped round his shoulders and head, partly to hide the sight of his mangled features, and partly to guard against erysipelas setting in through stray

Allen's face was smashed and mangled

particles of foreign matter getting into his wounds.

As for me, I walked calmly away with hardly a scratch on me; and for the next few weeks, until, in fact I returned to New York, I was the spoiled and flattered darling of New Orleans. The fair sex especially showered upon me all sorts of more or less embarrassing attentions, feeling my muscles and openly expressing their admiration for what they were pleased to term my 'fine physique' until - although I am not by any means a man of a particularly modest disposition naturally - I was fain to take refuge in flight.

I was now, of course, not only Champion of England, but also of America, which meant Champion of the World. But I soon found that the notoriety the position gave me was not going to add to the safety, let alone the pleasure, of living. New York was then about as 'tough' a place as it is possible to conceive of. Rows in the sporting houses on the Bowery and elsewhere were of daily occurrence. And whereas in England a row meant nothing worse, as a general rule, than a few hard blows given or received, rows in America meant almost invariably the drawing of pistols and knives, followed by the shedding of blood.

Nor was there any redress if one were attacked and injured. John Morrissey, an ex-prizefighter himself, and a former Mayor of New

York, was all-powerful in local politics still, so that no judge dared to go against his friends.

And as his friends included practically all the thugs and thieves of the city, the danger run by an outsider like myself, for instance, may be imagined.

For this reason I determined to quit New York, after more than one attempt had been made on my life for no other reason that I could see save that I was a 'darned Britisher' who had beaten America's adopted son in the prize ring. I travelled all through the Eastern States and met with a very varying, although on the whole not unkindly, reception. My boxing exhibitions were, however, well attended, so that I made plenty of money; which was, after all I reflected, the main thing.

When presently, too, I crossed over into Canada, my reception was a uniformly friendly one. In fact, in some of the places I visited, notably Quebec and Montreal, I found myself quite a lion.

It was in the former city, by the way, that I renewed my acquaintance with the Joe Wormald mentioned previously. He had come out to the New World in advance of me, and after drifting about the States for a while, had emigrated to Montreal, where he opened a boxing saloon, afterwards moving to Quebec.

Poor fellow! He had always had an idea that he was really a better man than I, and later on, after I had left Canada, he challenged me. I accepted, but the police interfered and no fight was possible although we had two separate tries. The disappointment brought on an illness which affected his brain, and he became a raving lunatic. His immense strength was so increased by his madness that he burst all ordinary bonds, and severely injured several of the attendants at the Marine Hospital, where he had been taken. As a result, they had to tie him hand and foot with new strong ropes, which, when he died, were buried with him.

Ned O' Baldwin, too, came to a sad end. Unlike me, he preferred to stay on in New York, and met with the fate that I consider would almost certainly have been mine had I consented to remain there, being shot and fatally wounded in a saloon row. Tom Allen, after his defeat by me, settled down in St. Louis, where he kept a big whisky store and sparring saloon, dying there of senile debility some few years ago.

But to return to the story of myself and my doings.

After touring Canada I returned to the States and New York, and presently I found myself challenged by Joe Coburn, the same man who had come over to England to fight me some six or seven years previously. I had no mind to meet him, not because I regarded him as at all a formidable opponent; but because I judged that there was little likelihood of the fight coming off after my experience with him in Ireland, as related in a previous chapter.

Besides, to tell the truth, I was frightened at what might happen to myself in the event of my winning - as I fully intended to do - supposing any chance the battle did come off.

This may sound strange talk, coming from me. But it is the truth. I did not fear violent knocks, but I did fear a violent death. And that is what a man risked who, being of British nationality, dared to do battle on American soil at that period with a Yankee pugilist.

I had it from Tom Allen's own lips, soon after my fight with him, that our battle at New Orleans was the most free from rowdyism or interference of any he had ever been present at in the States, whether as principal or spectator. He also showed me two bullet wounds on his body, inflicted by ring-side 'toughs' in a previous fight, when he had given battle, as an avowed Britisher, to a pugilist of American extraction.

Knowing these things, I made it clear to Coburn that any fight I might have with him must come off on British territory and eventually, after a lot of wrangling, Port Dover, Canada, was fixed upon, the stakes being £400. The date was the eleventh of May 1871, and as this was some months ahead, I utilised the interval to return to England and see to some business there that I had left in the hands of an agent and which required my personal attention.

On my return, I found all Canada and the United States talking of the match which, it was assured on all sides, would not be allowed to come off. And so, indeed, it proved for when we stepped into the ring a force of fully five hundred police appeared from an ambush and completely surrounded us.

To do battle with one and another under such circumstances would, of course, have been an act of extreme folly. For in Canada at that time, as also in the United States, a convicted prize-fighter was shown no mercy, sentences of eighteen months and two years' imprisonment being quite the usual thing.

Nevertheless, we sparred together for the better part of an hour, so as to give the spectators at least a show for their money. Then, in obedience to a strong hint from the inspector in charge of the constabulary, we took our departure.

Next day the referee ordered us to meet again on the eleventh of June at Kansas City. I duly put in an appearance, but Coburn stayed away, pleading illness. Naturally, I claimed the stakes, being fully entitled to them. But Harry Hill, the famous New York saloonkeeper, who was stake-holder, was threatened with death if he dared to hand over the money to the 'darned Britisher', and in the end we each received back the amount we had deposited.

A little while afterwards Coburn challenged me for the third and last time, the stakes being £1,200, the place, Bay St. Louis, in the state of Mississippi, and the date the thirtieth of November 1871. This time the battle did actually come off. But again my nationality prevented my getting fair play, for after we had fought twelve rounds, and just when it became evident that I had Master Joe hopelessly beaten, the referee, in obedience to the clamour and threats of as dangerous and bloodthirsty a mob as I had ever seen gathered round a ring, pronounced the fight a draw.

Disgusted and sore, I left the place of encounter with my friends. We had about an hour to wait at the station for a train to take us northward, and during that brief interval two separate attempts were made to shoot me, the would-be assassins concealing themselves in the cotton-fields by which the station buildings were surrounded. Luckily both bullets missed; but it was a near thing in one instance, at all events, the projectile striking the wall between Pooley and me as we were standing engaged in conversation not more than a foot or so apart.

After this disgraceful treatment, I let it be publicly known that I would accept no more challenges from Coburn, come what would, as I considered that I had already beaten him, but that I was open to do battle with any other pugilist of acknowledged repute.

The response to this came in due course, and from a most unexpected quarter. Ned O' Baldwin, the 'Irish Giant', who, but for police interference, I should have fought in England in 1867, threw down the gauntlet, and, of course, I had no choice but to accept.

This battle was to have come off on the 15th of July, 1872, in Virginia, and it had been arranged to proceed down the Ohio River by steamers, three of which had been specially chartered for the occasion. On the eve of the excursion, however, the captains of the boats were served by the authorities with warrants forbidding them to carry passengers who were about to commit a breach of the peace, so that affair was off.

Another attempt to hold a meeting on the following day was also frustrated by the police, and in the end the stakes were withdrawn. O' Baldwin went back to Quebec, and a few months afterwards was stricken down with the terrible malady which terminated his life, as already narrated.

Chapter 22
I Fight Davis Twice and leave America for Australia

So disgusted was I with these repeated fiascos, coupled with the despair I began to feel of ever getting fair play, that I determined to shake the dust of New York off my feet, my departure being hastened by the fact that certain friends of Coburn had openly avowed their intention of shooting me on sight. My first intention was to travel straight across the American continent to San Francisco, whence I intended taking ship to Australia. But on the eve of my departure I received an invitation of an entirely unexpected and most flattering nature from the inhabitants of Virginia City, Nevada.

This was nothing else than that I should visit them on my way west, and fight a battle to the finish with one Bill Davis, a pugilist of considerable local repute. Neither of us, it was explained, was to be called upon to put up any money, as a purse of £1,000 had been subscribed by the citizens of the place, to which also had been added a gold trophy belt, the gift of Mr. Mackay, the millionaire silver king.

Naturally such a bait was too tempting to be ignored. I telegraphed my willingness, and in due course the fight came off before a crowd of, I should think, fully ten thousand people. Contrary to my half-formed expectations, I was given perfectly fair play, and beat my opponent in thirty-two minutes.

The result, which was altogether unexpected locally, aroused tremendous excitement, and several revolver shots were fired by persons in the crowd. I do not think, however, that they were directed at me, being rather in the nature of an exhibition of exuberance of spirits by the wild western miners and cowboys who made up a considerable percentage of the spectators.

Indeed, I have nothing whatever to complain of as regards my treatment in Virginia City, or indeed throughout the Western States generally, where I was received with perfect courtesy, and treated in many instances with surprising kindness and hospitality. It was only in the Eastern States, and especially in New York, where the hostile Irish-American element ruled supreme, that I suffered persecution and injustice on account of my nationality.

Davis, too, took his licking well; and even went so far as to ask me if I would give him another opportunity by meeting him when I got to San Francisco, provided he, or his friends, could arrange for another purse, one-fourth to go to the loser and three-fourths to the winner. I was agreeable, and we met again in due course near that city, the amount of the purse being this time, however, reduced to £120.

It was rather a come-down after my Virginia City experience. But I had passed my word, so had to abide by it. And very glad I was in the end, for the number of people who flocked to see the match at a dollar a head for admission, and from five to fifty dollars for seats in the grand stand, was so great that my share of the gate money alone exceeded the sum for which I had fought in Nevada. And then I besides had the lion's share of the purse, for of course I beat Bill, who was nowhere near my form.

However, he was perfectly satisfied, for of course his share of the 'gate' was the same in amount as mine, and he was enabled with it to go back to Virginia City and start a saloon, which throve so exceedingly that he afterwards, I heard, became one of the leading men in the place, holding amongst other offices those of Mayor and Police Court Judge.

Meanwhile, I was *feted* and made much of in San Francisco, amongst other presents and tokens of goodwill I received during my stay being a solid silver brick, bearing this inscription: 'To James Mace, Champion of the World. Presented by the Miners of California. This is a brick, and you're another'.

But if the people of California were kind, those of Australia were enthusiasm personified. Everywhere I went on landing I was followed by cheering crowds, and my sparring exhibitions were so well attended that I made money hand-over-fist.

I was still open to meet all-comers with the gloves, but I had by this time made up my mind to engage in no more prize-fights. Indeed, in Australia any more than in England, it would not have been allowed.

On the other hand, there was no objection whatever raised to my boxing-booth, and I travelled with it for years up and down the country, penetrating into all sorts of out-of-the-way places in the wild 'back blocks' right up to the borders of the terrible 'Never Never Land' and the Great Central Desert.

The adventures that befell me during this period of my career alone would fill a good-sized volume, but space is limited. One, however, I cannot refrain from mentioning. It happened in New South Wales, and the year, I think, was 1879.

We were showing 'for one night only' at a little bush township, the name of which I cannot now recall and had just concluded our last performance, when a horseman cantered up - a big black-bearded chap - followed by three others, all of them being armed to the teeth. I noticed an uneasy movement amongst the crowd surrounding the booth, although no one spoke a word, and I thought I detected a sigh of relief when the big man, who appeared to be the leader, inquired for me by name.

I stepped forward, and civilly asked him his business. 'We want to see your show', he replied, adding that he and his companions had ridden forty miles for this purpose. I told him I was sorry, but that our regular evening performance was already finished, that both my men and myself were tired, and that it would be quite impossible to give a second show.

'Oh, stow your gab!' was his ungracious retort to my politely-worded excuses; 'I didn't ask for a speech, I asked to see your show. We want to see it, and what's more we mean to see it. So get a move on, and be quick about it. I'm not a man that's used to being trifled with. How much do you charge?'

'Ten pounds is the price for a private performance, which is what you are asking for', I told him.

'All right', he said; 'here's your money'-- handing me ten sovereigns; 'now get to work'.

Of course, after that there was no help for it. So we set to, and gave our regular show - boxing, wrestling, and so on, and all the while those four stern-visaged men sat silently watching. They never applauded, or showed any sign, save by the intensity of their gaze, that they were interested. But when it was all over the big-bearded man came and thanked me and shook hands with me. 'You're a celebrity, Mr. Mace', he said, his foot on the stirrup ready to mount and ride away, 'and so am I. We ought to be each of us proud to have met the other'.

'Who is he?' I asked, as the clatter of their horse's hoofs died away in the darkness.

'Ned Kelly', answered one of the crowd in a half-whisper, fearfully.

Then, of course, I knew, for the exploits of the famous bush-ranger were at that time the common talk of the Colony. He and his gang had held up banks, robbed stores, done battle with and killed the police officers sent against them, and generally terrorised a district half the size of England.

At that very moment, as everybody there was well aware, there was a Government reward of £10,000 out for him, dead or alive. Yet such was the fear he had contrived to instil into the hearts of those hardy bushmen, that not one of them dared lift a hand against him.

After I had done pretty well all Australia, I sailed for New Zealand, being presented on the eve of my departure with a belt of virgin gold mined on the spot. My reception on landing was as flattering as ever, and my tour resulted fully as well from a pecuniary point of view.

I was continually adding to my troupe of boxers as I journeyed from place to place, and amongst those I picked up was a young Maori half-breed named Slade. He was a magnificent athlete, and a quick and skilful boxer. His weight in fighting trim was two hundred and thirty-six pounds, and he stood six feet one and three-quarter inches in height.

At this time John L. Sullivan, the American 'slugger', was challenging the world with the gloves - prize-fights with the naked fists having been stopped altogether in America as elsewhere - and it occurred to me that Slade might stand a chance against him. The young Maori was quite willing, so I set to work to train him, imparting to him all the ring-craft of which I was master, after which we sailed for San Francisco, whence we journeyed by easy stages to New York, giving exhibitions at the different towns we stopped at on the way.

The match came off in the Madison Square Garden, New York, in the summer of 1883, and excited an enormous amount of interest, the vast building being packed at two dollars a seat for the common seats, the place altogether holding some twenty thousand dollars - a nice little sum for Sullivan, Slade, and myself to split up between us. As for the fight, however, that was a disappointing affair from my point of view, the Maori being altogether 'out of it' when confronted with the gigantic Irish-American blacksmith.

Had he won, I should have kept him with me, and he would have been, without doubt, a fine drawing card for my show. But after his defeat he was practically of no use to me, so I let Sullivan have him, and he took him touring through the Eastern States, while I moved 'down south', so that our exhibitions might not clash with one another. I visited practically every town in the south and west, sometimes performing in a booth, sometimes in barns and such like buildings, but more often in music halls and theatres. Everywhere we were well received, the early prejudice against Britishers appearing to have died out.

Nevertheless, there came a time at last when I grew tired of wandering in an alien land, and turned my steps to my own country.

I have tried my hand at several kinds of business since my arrival, but in the end I have invariably returned to my first love, the circus and the boxing booth. Only there, now that old age has come upon me, do I feel really at home.

Many a time I have been asked by friends and acquaintances to give it up. They tell me that when a man is seventy-seven it is time he took a rest.

But I do not agree with them. I have boxed my way more than half round the world and back again, and in every town, and in pretty well every village in England. And I intend to keep on at it till the end.

I was at Fun City, Olympia, last Christmas, with my booth and my troupe of boxers, and I hope to be there next Christmas if I am spared. I am dictating these closing words of my story behind the scenes of a circus, and as I pause for a moment I hear the ringmaster announcing that 'Jem Mace, the retired Champion of the World, will now spar a few exhibition rounds'. And then he goes on to recount my triumphs. It is sweet music to my ears.

Some day, soon of course, I shall be challenged by an adversary whom there will be no gainsaying, to fight my last battle, a battle without either seconds or backers or referee, and the result of which will be a foregone conclusion.

Well, I trust I shall be given strength and courage to toe the scratch without flinching, and to face him with a bold front. I know I shall try to. For what use is it to show the white feather, even to Death?

After all, he can but knock me out.

Afterword

And so ends the life story of the great Jem Mace...or at least as much of Jem's tale as could be easily condensed between two covers to tell of his busy life both in and out of the ring. Although Mace's memoirs suggest that his career more or less drew to a close, with his globetrotting ending following his journey from Australia back to America and his subsequent return home to England, the final couple of pages roughly summarizing Jem's movements after this time actually cover a period of no less than twenty five years, and further voyages across the sea. Mace dictated his story to journalists in 1908, a full quarter of a century after his return to the land of his birth, when he was seventy seven years of age, and one of the last of the old bare knuckle breed then living.

Fifty Years a Fighter records Mace's thoughts and memories from his childhood days throughout his fighting career up until his return to Great Britain in 1883. The text comprises Jem Mace's own personal recollections, and told in his own words. It is almost unique as a document, as it is not a story composed by the pens of biographers through close study of newspaper articles covering the career highlights of a long retired prize fighter, but a firsthand account of one of the foremost ring men of his time, chronicling the final death throes of the English prize ring. At one time the spectacle of a prize fight had been celebrated at almost every level of British society, although as can be seen from Mace's account of his fighting days, the ring had long since fallen from grace and into disrepute.

Like many of his time, Jem's early days were not spent confined to a classroom and a formal education, but in pursuit of a trade, firstly as an apprentice blacksmith, and then as a cabinet maker. Consequently, Mace in his own words '...never had any book learning to speak of'. Being unable to write down his story, the elderly pugilist was forced to dictate his tale, with Mace's speech having been recorded by his biographers. While he was hampered by his lack of schooling his whole life, throughout his story Jem Mace proves himself to be a shrewd and intelligent man, with a natural charisma and flair for telling a tale.

His educational shortcomings were a sensitive matter for Jem, who often felt frustrated at the necessity for his thoughts and words to be recorded by others, despite having been in possession of a keen mind. Additional upset was also caused by the continual insistence that he was of Romany gypsy origin,

Jem Mace in 1862 after his 2nd fight with Tom King

often having been referred to by the ring name of the 'Swaffham Gypsy' by both his supporters and detractors alike.

The very first page of his memoirs seeks to dispel this commonly held 'fact', with Mace stating that the notion that he was a gypsy stemmed from the association with his uncle Barney, and his cousin and close companion, Pooley Mace. Pooley's mother had been a gypsy girl whom Uncle Barney had met and married at Norwich Fair. As Jem and Pooley were often in each other's company, this resulted in a situation where Pooley's gypsy origins were often confused with those of Jem, - or at least if Jem is to be believed in any case.

After having both made and lost a fortune in the prize ring, Jem engaged a supposed expert to draw up a chart of his family tree, and in later years is said to have carried it about with him as a matter of course. Jem alleged that this chart proved that he could trace his ancestors back over three centuries; with the majority being rustic 'tradesmen' of purely English descent, such as wheelwrights, carpenters and blacksmiths, as his father, a blacksmith, was before him. Some probably thought understandably enough, that Mace himself protested a little 'too much', but naturally didn't press the champion pugilist too hard on this point. In any case, the name stayed, even if in time it ended up being shortened to 'the Gypsy'.

Any mention of 'the Gypsy' would ensure that the chart would be quickly produced, rapidly unrolled, and the origin of his ring name verbally disputed by Jem Mace at some length, while also revealing the extensive tree of names of his forefathers, thus proving that he was of solidly 'English' stock.

Whether there was any gypsy blood in Mace's family line is difficult to prove or not, although it must be said that Mace showed all the inclinations of the Romany people that he refused to accept as his personal kin. While Jem enjoyed the company of travelling people, and spent much of his life around show people and travelling folk, he refuted the suggestion that he had any gypsy blood in his background until the end of his days. His love of music and dancing, his relentless pursuit of adventure, and his tireless wandering also served to lend credence to the notion that he was a gypsy, in his nature and inclinations at least, in the minds of many.

It is likely that Mace's refusal to admit any gypsy background may have been in part due to the manner in which the Romany people had been viewed and treated in Mace's time, having been frequently associated with the criminal classes and often viewed with suspicion in the minds of the general public. By the time Jem Mace told his story his name had figured in thousands of newspaper column inches in virtually every newspaper of note in Britain and beyond. At times he had been showered with glory, but had also been the recipient of sharply worded criticism – so much so following his inability to appear for his fight against Mike Madden, that he had been depicted as a 'coward' and 'cur' in so influential a newspaper as *Bell's Life in London*. This criticism had created such a surge of public condemnation and rage that a mob tried to burn down Mace's Norwich home.

Mace had no desire to be painted as any more of a villain than he already had been in the newspapers following press reports on various 'scandalous' aspects of his personal life outside the ring, and for this reason probably chose to disassociate himself from his connections with the gypsy community as much as possible.

The last significant event that Mace records in his memoirs prior to his return to England is his decision to take Herbert Slade, 'the Maori', to the United States to fight against John L. Sullivan. Although Mace's recollections gloss over the issue, the decision to serve Slade up against such a formidable opponent as the American champion was supremely ill-judged and cost Mace dearly. Money had been at the heart of the decision to promote Slade, with Mace seeking to make a quick and substantial profit by presenting the exotic New Zealander as a worthy opponent for Sullivan, whilst privately knowing that his protégé was completely

Mace in the US in 1877 before leaving for Australia

unsuited to the task. Mace had found Slade when he was little more than a rank amateur as a fighter, and having trained him in the basics, misguidedly promoted him as a tremendous talent based on little more than his physically imposing frame and a rudimentary knowledge of wrestling. Inevitably Slade was defeated with laughable ease, and while this cast a shadow over Mace's reputation in the short-term, his own legacy as a fighter remained undamaged.

Following his return to the United Kingdom, Mace initially settled in Liverpool, the hometown of his wife, Nellie. No doubt seeking to distance himself from the public disapproval that had previously occurred as a result of press scrutiny into his tangled personal life, Mace makes markedly little reference to his doings outside the ring in the course of his memoirs. This in itself is somewhat understandable, Nellie was the *fourth* woman to bear the *ninth* of Mace's children; Mace's love-life was the subject of many column inches in the popular press, and had led to him being judged as a scoundrel by many. Regardless, this negative publicity would appear to have left Mace's life-long love of women undimmed, with his charismatic personality ensuring that he would go on to have a further *five* children with one Alice Stokes, an eighteen year old barmaid from Glasgow, whom Mace had met when performing in the Scottish city when Mace was nearly sixty!

Despite having earned a substantial amount of money from his career in the ring, and his countless exhibition matches and paid appearances, Mace had throughout his days of glory been careless in the handling of his finances. While fighting in the prize ring Mace had made a sizable proportion of his money from gambling on himself to win. His gambling grew in proportion to his means, and after reaching the heights of his fame he continued to enjoy gambling on the racecourses of the mining towns of Australia for even higher stakes, and even went so far as to invest in his own racehorses. On his return to England, he continued to lose heavily on the horses, although this would seem to be an effort to dispel the tedium of his semi-retirement following his withdrawal from professional prize-fighting.

Inevitably, given his roving nature, Mace could not resist the forbidden excitement and allure of the prize ring for long. He soon invested in a pub in the East end of London, where he hoped to discover the English heavyweight champions of the future. Mace had found on his return that the current crop of English heavyweights had deteriorated massively in comparison to the skills of their predecessors, with top class men like Tom King and Bob Travers having being replaced by altogether less skillful performers such as Jem Smith.

Jem Smith had risen to the top of a limited pool of domestic talent chiefly through his great strength and power. While his bulk and obvious muscularity had caused many to fear the strength of the ex-Shoreditch labourer, his boxing skills were distinctly lacking, and Smith frequently relied on questionable roughhouse tactics in order to secure victory. Jem Mace viewed Smith with little more than barely concealed contempt, often remarking that Jem Smith's bulky and immobile weightlifters frame was something more akin to a 'bullock' than Mace's idea of a true fighting man.

For these reasons, Jem found himself at the centre of efforts to revive the days of the old prize ring in December of 1885, when one Jack Davis was chosen as the opponent for Smith in a battle for the heavyweight championship of England. Mace chose to put his support behind Davis and seconded him against the musclebound Smith. To Mace's great disappointment, when faced by Smith's hulking frame, Davis lost his nerve and ended up getting mercilessly pummelled into submission before the appearance of the police forced Mace and the other spectators to flee the scene of battle. This, and similar disappointments would lead Mace to conclude in the course of his memoirs that, 'Prize fighting in England has been dead....for these forty years and more, and there is an end to it....Under present conditions it would be manifestly impossible to revive it. And, even if it were not impossible, I am of the opinion that it would be eminently undesirable.'

With so little talent to be found, the retired champion wound up his interests in the London public house, although his desire to discover and foster the champions of tomorrow remained even into the final years of his life. This possibility had been a focus of Jem's activities since his days in Australia, where Mace had popularized glove fighting as an alternative to the knuckles. Through his efforts he would also play a pivotal role in bringing the first crop of Australian boxers to reach global fame to the attention of the world.

The very brief account of Mace's five year stay in Australia contained within *'Fifty Years a Fighter'*, which only contains one quickly recounted meeting with the famous outlaw Ned Kelly, does not reflect the impact that Mace's years in the country would have on the developing sport of Australian boxing, then in its infancy. Nor does the picture of Mace being sat on a wagon bouncing its way through dusty outback towns as far as '...the borders of the terrible 'Never Never Land' and the Grand Central Desert' accurately record the true scale and significance of Mace's Australian adventure, or its resultant impact on world boxing. Neither does it fully do justice to the heights to which the name of Jem Mace had now risen, with Mace having now been viewed as the legitimate Champion of the World after his destruction of both Tom Allen and Joe Coburn in the United States.

After arriving in Australia, Mace had made money hand over fist. A young man from Bathurst in New South Wales named Larry Foley had awaited Mace's arrival with particular interest. Foley approached Jem and asked if he might tutor him in the art of boxing. The Australian was not entirely green when it came to prize-fighting, having fought seventy one rounds in a bitterly contested prize-fight when just seventeen years old. Seeing Larry's raw bravery, Mace elected to take him in hand, with Foley having been instructed at 'Mace's Athletic Hall' in Melbourne, and afterwards receiving a further education while fighting on Mace's boxing booth as it toured the country. Larry Foley blossomed under Mace's care to such a degree that he went on to beat Abe Hicken on the 20th March 1879, and was afterwards considered as the Champion of Australia. Mace put down temporary roots in Melbourne, and bought a share in a hotel, and soon found that he had enough money to squander on gambling on horse racing. Larry Foley more wisely used his winnings from the fight with Hicken to open a public house. It was from here, at the White Horse in Sydney, where Foley also gave boxing lessons, that a golden age of Australian boxers would issue forth.

In uncovering and developing new talent, Foley was very successful, and diligently taught his pupils all of the ring craft that he had learned from Mace. Bill Murphy, a tailor by trade from Auckland in New Zealand had been discovered by Mace, and afterwards sent to Foley for instruction. Murphy received such expert tuition that he went on to defeat Ike Weir in San Francisco, and became the first Australian fighter to seize a world title.

Murphy was afterwards dethroned by another of Larry's discoveries, the legendary Albert Griffiths, in the first world title fight to be held in Australia. Griffiths, who became known to the world as 'Young Griffo', was a newspaper seller from one of the roughest part of Sydney, and had been spotted by Foley when scrapping in a street fight. Impressed by his obvious toughness, Larry decided to give young Albert lessons in the 'scientific' art of boxing as taught to him by Jem Mace.

'Griffo' was in possession of almost freakish abilities, and had reflexes so sharp that he was able to catch a fly in mid air between his fourth finger and thumb. He was also blessed with sublime defensive skills. One of Young Griffo's party-tricks was to stand within the confines of a handkerchief placed on the floor, and successfully dodge all punches thrown at him through movement of just his head and his hips alone.

Another of Foley's talents was Peter Jackson, a ship hand from the West Indian island of St. Croix, and arguably the most significant of

Larry's discoveries. Jackson had travelled to Australia in search of opportunity, and had shown such natural talent at boxing that he had been introduced to Foley on his arrival in Australia. Even at nineteen years old Jackson had an imposing physique. Standing a shade under 6 foot 2 inches, he had unusual athletic grace for a man of his size. Noting the untrained natural power that Jackson was able to inject into his punching, Foley sent for Mace, hoping to get the old master's verdict on his new prospect. The first introduction that Jackson would receive in boxing was through watching Larry Foley spar against the veteran Champion of the World.

Peter Jackson proved to be a dedicated pupil under Foley's tutelage, and took the Australian Heavyweight title in 1886. The 'Black Prince' afterwards travelled to the United States taking all that he had learned of the Mace 'method' in his luggage, and quickly established himself as one of the greatest fighters of his generation, defeating such notables as George Godfrey, Joe McAuliffe and Patsy Cardiff. Peter would have been the natural choice to fight for world honours had it not been for John L. Sullivan's refusal to meet any black challengers in the ring.

With the hope that public pressure would force Sullivan to reconsider his position, Jackson travelled to England to meet the cumbersome English champion, Jem Smith, who was decisively outclassed within just two rounds, much to the delight of Jem Mace himself. Although now considered amongst the front runners of those deserving the right to challenge Sullivan for his crown, Jackson's claim was ignored, making him one of the most gifted fighters down the ages to have never been given the opportunity to fight for a world title. That Jackson was the best candidate for the job seems indisputable, having fought Sullivan's eventual conqueror, Jim Corbett to a sixty one round draw in San Francisco in May of 1891.

Having firmly sown the seeds of boxing greatness in Australia, and left the subsequent crop to be nurtured and harvested by the patient hand of Larry Foley, Jem Mace travelled to New Zealand. It was here that he promoted 'Jem Mace' amateur boxing competitions, where local talent could compete for small cups presented by Mace, and win the right to spar a few rounds with the master himself. In this way, Mace continued to foster the art of boxing even in this far-off land.

It was at Timaru that Mace came across a young blacksmith whose power and hitting abilities were so great that Mace felt that he had stumbled upon a special talent. The blacksmith's name was Bob Fitzsimmons, and he would in time become both middleweight and heavyweight champion of the world. That Bob would appear to have been earmarked for greatness had been apparent from the beginning. 'Fitz' knocked out four men in one night for the prize of a gold watch and the right to call himself the amateur champion of New Zealand – at a Jem Mace boxing competition held in his hometown in 1883. Young Bob Fitzsimmons had been born in Helston, Cornwall before having emigrated to New Zealand with his family as a boy. Fitzsimmons would reign as the last British born Heavyweight Champion of the World until Lennox Lewis over a century later.

Mace's influence on the development of British boxing was also considerable. Within a decade after his return, the National Sporting Club had been founded in London in 1891. Both directly and indirectly the fighting career of Jem Mace had impacted upon its most important members. John Fleming had founded the club, and had been a frequent visitor to Nat Langham's public house, the 'Cambrian Stores' and heard tales of Langham's glory days when the retired middleweight champion had run the famous Rum-pum-pas Club and aristocrats had dined at their leisure and afterwards watched men fight with the knuckles. Inspired by Langham's success, it was Fleming that proved the driving force in founding a modern version of the Rum-pum-pas Club where 'gentlemen' could eat, drink and make merry and watch a glove contest from the comfort of padded seats in a well lit converted theatre.

The most significant of the N.S.C. committee members was Hugh Cecil Lowther, who would become better known as Lord Lonsdale, one of the most notable public figures to lend his support to the sport of gloved boxing after the decline of the prize ring. Lonsdale's love of the noble art had been fostered when he was a boy, through his tuition in the sport by no less a master than Jem Mace himself. Hugh had proved to be an unruly child and one fond of fighting with other boys, and so his father decided his energies might be better controlled through a practical course of boxing instruction. With a vast personal fortune at his disposal it proved no great difficulty for Hugh's father to secure the services of Jem Mace for a period of time. The tuition resulted in a lifelong respect for Mace and his boxing abilities and a love of pugilism that would make the name of 'Lonsdale' forever afterwards associated with the history of British boxing.

The man responsible for the day to day running of the National Sporting Club was one Arthur F. Bettinson, who had been an outstanding all-round sportsman in his youth and an excellent amateur boxer, having taken the lightweight amateur title in 1882. Bettinson was certainly one of Mace's most ardent supporters, having studied Jem's ring career for many years, and finally concluded that there was just one style of boxing, and that the most 'perfect exponent' of this style was none other than Jem Mace.

National Sporting Club members got the opportunity to see Mace within the ring in 1894 when Mace had graced the boxing theatre with a demonstration of his style, although he was now sixty three years of age. One night early in October of 1895, Mace ducked between the ropes once more to meet Dick Burge, who was over thirty years younger than the ring veteran. Burge was astonished to find that Mace managed to dodge many of his blows, and that the elderly pugilist was still exceptionally quick and nimble for his years and still fit enough to see out a three round exhibition with one of the leading lightweights in the country. Realizing they had witnessed something special, at the end of his performance the audience to a man rose and gave Mace a deafening applause.

That there was plenty of fire left in the veteran fighter had been made apparent a few years previously by his surprising decision to engage Charlie Mitchell in a four round contest in Glasgow in 1890. Jem's deteriorating finances had prompted the meeting, with the wily pugilist laying bets on himself to see out the four two minute rounds without having been knocked either down or out. While police interference in the final round brought the fight to an early end, much to Mace's annoyance, Jem had been well on his way to a decent pay day. It is astonishing to relate that he was fifty eight years old – and meeting a highly regarded opponent in Mitchell, who less than two years previously had fought John L. Sullivan to a draw.

Highpoints aside, Mace was struggling to keep his head above water throughout the 1890's, having been declared bankrupt in 1894. The following year found him at the National Sporting Club in Covent Garden, although on this occasion he did not appear in the ring, having been forced to accept the offer of the use of the premises to sell the numerous cups, belts and prizes commemorating the victories of his long fighting career in the hope of paying off his debt. In 1896 he travelled back to America, taking up an earlier missed opportunity to meet the celebrated American boxing instructor 'Professor' Mike Donovan, in a match billed for the Veteran's Championship of the World, at the invitation of the Broadway Athletic Club in New York. As twenty years had passed since he had last been in the country, there were no great crowds waiting for him as he stepped off the gangplank, although fighting men and boxing enthusiasts by the score had awaited his arrival and waited in turn to shake him by the hand.

Donovan had been nervous about the meeting, despite being sixteen years younger than the old warhorse. Feeling that he needed someone of first rate ability to work his corner, Donovan spoke to Joe Choynski, one of the most prominent American heavyweights, having met the Heavyweight Champion, 'Gentleman' Jim Corbett on three separate occasions in his

Jem in New York 1896

youth. Choynski later spoke of his recollection of Donovan's concerns to a newspaper, with Mike having anxiously confided in him;

> "This Mace is the greatest boxer who ever lived. I am not afraid of getting hurt. I can take a beating if I have to. But this is my home town and I have a reputation. Suppose Mace would make a fool of me." [1]

Despite Mike Donovan's nervousness, the manner in which both men finally met bore testament not only to the regard with which the American fighting fraternity remembered Mace's impact on the sport, but also to the good natured charm and courtesy of the aging boxer. Not that Mace's age was easily guessed, with one newspaper stating that he had *'devoted himself to the gentle art of how to grow old and look young,'* and that *'...he is as great a master at this as he was at his earlier art of putting men to sleep with his fists.'* [2]

Spotting Mike Donovan coming to greet him, Mace smiled broadly and shook his hand warmly, exclaiming "well, Mike, old boy, how in the world are you? How've you been, eh?" Donovan was said to have been so happy that his face displayed 'about six smiles' on it. The

---

[1] *The Advertiser (Australia) February 1st, 1927 - 'The Days of Finish Fights' No. XXVI*
[2] *The World (USA) 23rd November, 1896 – Jem Mace and Donovan, Veterans of the Ring*

rest of their meeting pays ample testament to the respect felt by each man for his opponent;

'The two leaned back in their chairs and smiled at each other. Their glances darted from point to point. Moved by some sudden impulse, each half rose and grasped the other's hand. Then they sat down again and studied each other keenly. Both men are a fine example of the healthy influence that hard fighting has upon a man. Both have eyes keen as a lynx. Mace's dark skin shows a ruddy tinge on the cheeks that a society bud might envy. Donovan's fair complexion is like a baby's.

"A little thin up there, Mike," Mace remarked as he stretched out his gnarled brown hand and patted Donovan's gray thatch. "Excuse, me, Jim," retorted Donovan, reaching over and deftly whipping off the Englishman's shining top hat, there stood revealed a dark, glistening bald poll. There was a roar of laughter from the admiring circle. The two veterans chaffed each other like boys. Their conversation was a pleasant reminder of by-gone days when pugilists used to ratify their matches in courteous phrases and then solemnly drink to the toast "May the best man win," each, of course, thinking of himself, but neither uttering a word to the other's disparagement.'

The contest between Mace and Donovan took place on December 14th 1896, with the verdict having been given as a draw by a majority of spectators, out of a desire to pay respectful tribute to the skills of both men. At sixty five, no-one was under any illusion that Mace could conceivably be the force that he had been over thirty years previously when he had been at his fighting prime. Joe Choynski would always remember the figure that Mace had cut in the ring that night, with the ex-Champion of the World having fought a winning battle against his advancing years. Speaking about the occasion over thirty years later, Choynski recalled;

'I was amazed when Jem Mace walked into the ring to see a man with coal black hair and with a body as smooth and plump as a man of thirty. Mace was a gipsy. I would like to know where he picked up his marvelous boxing skill....in action he was graceful, resourceful and fast. Donovan scarcely laid a glove on him squarely. Mace's head shifting was marvelously timed. He could gauge distance and slip blows by a hair. Here was Griffo and Corbett and Fitzsimmons and Jim Hall all combined into one'.
3

Perhaps the most significant moment of Mace's third journey to America occurred after his match with Mike Donovan when the English champion met for the second time with Jim Corbett, the very first Champion of the World under Marquis of Queensberry Rules. Corbett

---

[3] *The Advertiser (Australia) February 1st, 1927 - 'The Days of Finish Fights' No. XXVI*

was also greatly impressed by Mace's skills after a friendly spar with the veteran, commenting;

> 'We boxed two two-minute rounds, and the old fellow really surprised me...he is great on straight left leads, and counters with a shifting of the head to the right. Mace is also very good with the old straight cross-counter, with the head shifted to the left, and his ducking is simply marvelous. He is very fast with his leads and has much quickness that more than surprised me. His ducking is simply wonderful for a man of his age. Of course, his strength leaves him after boxing with a big, vigorous, strong man, but with an opponent not so strong and vigorous he will make it very interesting...Mace's wind is very good, and after our bout was over he had not turned a hair.' [4]

The two men afterwards posed for photographs together, and were captured for prosperity shaking gloved hands with one another in a richly historic sporting image. As the first true world boxing champion under modern rules, Mace retained a respect for Jim Corbett which few heavyweight boxers of his time would equal. Corbett in turn always acknowledged that it had been Jem Mace's pioneering spirit that had laid the foundation stones for the development and evolution of the sport of boxing.

---

[4] *The World (USA) 23rd November, 1896 – Jem Mace and Donovan, Veterans of the Ring*

Jem Mace & Jim Corbett

Mace afterwards returned to England, having received somewhere in the region of $2,000 for his share of the proceeds for the meeting with Donovan according to Choynski's recollections. Mace had been overwhelmed by the presentation of the funds and reportedly cried tears of gratitude. Despite the fanfare which still greeted his appearance in the US, Mace found that his glory had faded in his own country, and he needed a regular source of income.

Finding that a sporting public house in Birmingham needed a new landlord, Mace applied. It was a lucky break. The brewery decided that a name so steeped in ring glory as that of Jem Mace could only help to attract greater custom, and gave Mace the job. He settled, as much as he could, at the Black Lion for a few years, although his roving nature could not be suppressed, and he found it difficult to settle into a life that did not feature boxing at its centre. Hoping to find a better life for himself and his family, and one in which he might still manage to unearth possible talent to mould into the great fighters of tomorrow, Mace decided that his future lay in South Africa. The decision to move there at the age of seventy two in the latter part of 1903 would prove disastrous.

On his arrival he had opened a boxing academy in Cape Town, but it had proved to be a disappointing failure. With the country still recovering from the Boer War, Mace found there was little interest in the sport amongst its people, and the school closed down within two months. Further journeys to America and Australia mopped up what little money he had left and he returned to Britain with barely a penny to his name. In the years that followed the retired champion became more and more dependent on the charity of friends, and desperately sought to avoid ending up in the workhouse. Despite this spiral into poverty, Mace's vigour was still plain to see on the occasions when he demonstrated his boxing skills.

One event when Jem dazzled an audience with his fighting abilities was at an evening at the Horns in Kennington in 1905 when he sparred with Wolf Bendoff, the Jewish middleweight. Prior to the event, few had guessed that the kindly looking old gentleman at the ringside had been none other than Jem Mace, retired champion pugilist of the world;

'Snow white curls rippled from beneath his glossy silk hat and a diamond pin of dazzling splendor illuminated even the brightness of his crimson tie. A long fawn overcoat covered a pair of massive shoulders and half-concealed his immaculate flannel trousers. The elderly gentleman seemed to have no object in life but to smile in a kindly way upon the world.

Presently he arose and walked with somewhat aged footsteps onto the stage and passed through a little door. Anon he reappeared, and so changed was he that one could scarcely recognize him...the elderly gentleman stood forth, stripped, with a gnarled neck and long, strong arms, upon which the muscles stood out like whipcord. But he still smiled in a most benign and grandfatherly way.' [5]

Although the first round was fought at a brisk pace, despite his age, Jem Mace appeared as game as ever, and implored Bendoff in the latter stages of the first round to hit harder, murmuring;

"*Hit harder, boy, hit harder! I've a hard old nut, and a hard old heart. Hit Harder!*"

Bendoff did punch harder, and Mace harder still in the second round, to rapturous applause from the audience. The third round showed to what an incredible degree Mace was able to turn back the years after entering the boxing ring, with an enthusiastic audience cheering him on;

'*At the beginning of the third round the boxing grandfather came up gamely and smiling more benignly than ever. The gnarled old arms flashed and twinkled and hit and parried and countered with the swiftness of a motor car and the strength of a traction engine. Blows fell upon the grand old arched chest, but Jem Mace did not*

---

[5] *The Saint Paul Globe (USA) April 23rd, 1905 – Veteran Jem Mace Fast With Gloves*

seem to feel them, and at the end of the final round he shook hands with his opponent, blew kisses with his gloved hands, and then skipped off the stage with the air of a kitten which had been toying with a mouse.' [6]

If any other evidence of the vigor with which Mace greeted old age is necessary, he had also become a father again at the age of seventy three with the birth of his daughter, Ellen, the fourteenth of his children, just nine weeks before.

Although Mace wanted to set himself up as a boxing instructor, he lacked the funds to do so, and would return to the fairground to make a slender living introducing a troupe of his boxers on his own booth, taking on all comers, just as he had done at Norwich Fair over half a century before when he had been little more than a boy. It is to be wondered if he regretted his decision to leave America, where his cousin Pooley had settled. Certainly his fame in the US was still such that he could have made a profitable living by either selling his recollections to the newspapers, or by proffering his opinions on the merits and drawbacks of the fighters of the day.

With each year pushing Mace's fighting career further into sporting history, Mace's money making opportunities declined as time went by. An opportunity to appear on the bill of

---

[6] *The Saint Paul Globe (USA) April 23rd, 1905 – Veteran Jem Mace Fast With Gloves*

Mace with Sam Langford the Canadian born pugilist in 1907

a small circus was gratefully received, and the magical name of Jem Mace, ex-champion of the world painted on a board outside the tent was still enough to encourage a few punters to part with their entrance money to see the grand old man of the ring. In a manner of speaking, Mace's journey had come full circle, and he now earned a crust through his violin, playing short pieces for the entertainment of the crowd, and occasionally appearing in theatrical turns, often as a veteran pugilist. To supplement his slender income, he could also be found busking his way round the pubs of the towns the circus was visiting, just as he had when as a fresh faced young lad he had first taken to the road in search of fame and fortune.

With nothing more than a draughty caravan to call home, the travelling life must have proved arduous and hard on the health of the elderly fighter. All of his material possessions had long since been sold to pay off his debts. There were only two items that Jem could not bear to part with even in his twilight years, one was his treasured violin, with the other being a small bust of his one-time great rival Tom Sayers, who had died some forty years previously. Mace retained enormous respect for the deceased champion, often stating his hope that he would be buried alongside Sayers when his time came.

Despite the poverty which accompanied his final days, Mace remained upbeat and cheerful,

Mace with a horseshoe given to him in 1909 by his pupil Bob Fitzsimmons

and though lameness had ensured that his final entrance into the ring occurred in October of 1909 at the age of seventy eight, the public still wished to gaze upon the face of Jem Mace, no longer hoping to witness a display of combative brilliance as they once had, but content merely to look upon one who represented the last of his pugilistic line. In November of 1910, Mace appeared at St. James Hall in Newcastle, and crowds were reported by the *World's Fair* journal to have flocked there wishing to see one thing;

'*...all they wanted was to see and hear the unconquered champion of the world. Their sole ambition was to gaze upon the veteran of the pugilistic ring, so that every day and every performance throughout the week the standing order in this world-famous establishment was either standing room only or house full.*'

It was at Jarrow where Mace had been attending the Fair with his circus troupe that his steadily declining health finally gave out following a chill that had weakened him considerably. On the 30th November 1910, Jem Mace passed away having outlived virtually all of his contemporaries.

After news had reached the ears of the newspaper men, obituaries were written, duplicated and re-written in virtually every corner of the globe. In America, where he had left such a credible legacy, reporters were keen to find an angle that would demonstrate the impact that Mace had left on his beloved sport of boxing. Hiram B. Cook had been the referee in the sixty one round match between Peter Jackson and James J. Corbett, and in his time at the California Athletic Club had seen most of the big names demonstrate their skills inside the ring, still Cook believed that not one of them could hold a candle to Mace, stating that;

"Mace was the most beautiful boxer I have ever seen in the ring. He was quick, scientific, and wonderful to behold. I would rather see Jem Mace in one three-minute round than anyone else I have ever watched for twenty rounds."[7]

Equally sorrowful at the loss of the great pugilist was the 'Belfast Chicken', Billy Clarke, who had been Mace's trainer when Jem had been engaged to fight Mike Madden fifty two years previously. Mace's decision to instead spend the evening chasing a 'pretty little barmaid' had led to an almighty bust up, with Mace's name having been dragged through the mud for cowardice after his subsequent drunkenness had prevented him appearing on the day of battle. In the years that had followed, Clark had moved to St. Louis in Missouri, and met the passing of his old friend with genuine regret;

"When 'Jem' and I met we were two little lads, but we knew how to land a good blow and

---

[7] *The Evening Bulletin (Honolulu) December 10th, 1910 – Tributes to Old Champion*

win a fight. I became a boxer because I had to support my mother and her six children. Jem was a natural-born fighter, so we tied up for two years. He knew more about boxing than any man on earth except me, because I learned all he ever knew before we were together a week. We had a rule for boxing. It was to land a lefthander at the right time and in the right place. That's how we won."[8]

Despite all that Mace had achieved within his lifetime, no memorial would mark his grave, and his final resting place in Anfield Cemetery in Liverpool seemed destined to be forever marked by a simple stone bearing nothing more than a plot number. Though subscriptions for a headstone that would adequately reflect the importance of his life and deeds were collected shortly after his death by *'Boxing'* magazine, the fund would appear to have failed, and his grave remained more or less forgotten in the decades that followed.

In 2002, over ninety years later, due to the fundraising efforts of the Merseyside Ex-Boxers Association, a black granite stone was finally erected on Jem Mace's grave. That Mace was finally remembered and his glories recalled by fellow pugilists and practitioners of the sport to which he had given so much, nearly a century after his death, would almost certainly have

---

[8] *The Evening Bulletin (Honolulu) December 10th, 1910 – Tributes to Old Champion*

made the old warrior's beatific smile beam out once more.

Lawrence Davies